THE **WORLD'S WORST** ASSISTANT

THE **WORLD'S WORST** ASSISTANT

Sona Movsesian

PLUME

PLUME
An imprint of Penguin Random House LLC
penguinrandomhouse.com

LIBRARY OF CONGRESS CATALOGING-IN-PUBLICATION DATA
Names: Movsesian, Sona, author.
Title: The world's worst assistant / Sona Movsesian.
Description: New York : Plume, [2022] Identifiers: LCCN 2022017150 (print) | LCCN 2022017151 (ebook) | ISBN 9780593185513 (hardcover) | ISBN 9780593185537 (ebook)
Subjects: LCSH: Movsesian, Sona. | O'Brien, Conan—Friends and associates. | Television broadcasting—United States—Biography. | Administrative assistants—Californina—Los Angeles—Biography. | LCGFT: Autobiographies.
Classification: LCC PN1992.4.M69 A3 2022 (print) | LCC PN1992.4.M69 (ebook) | DDC 791.4302/32092 [B]—dc23/eng/20220414
LC record available at https://lccn.loc.gov/2022017150
LC ebook record available at https://lccn.loc.gov/2022017151

Printed in the United States of America
10 9 8 7 6 5 4 3 2 1

BOOK DESIGN BY ASHLEY TUCKER

For my little gentlemen, Charlie and Mikey,
I hope you don't inherit my work ethic.
And to Tak, I couldn't have written this without you.
I love my guys.

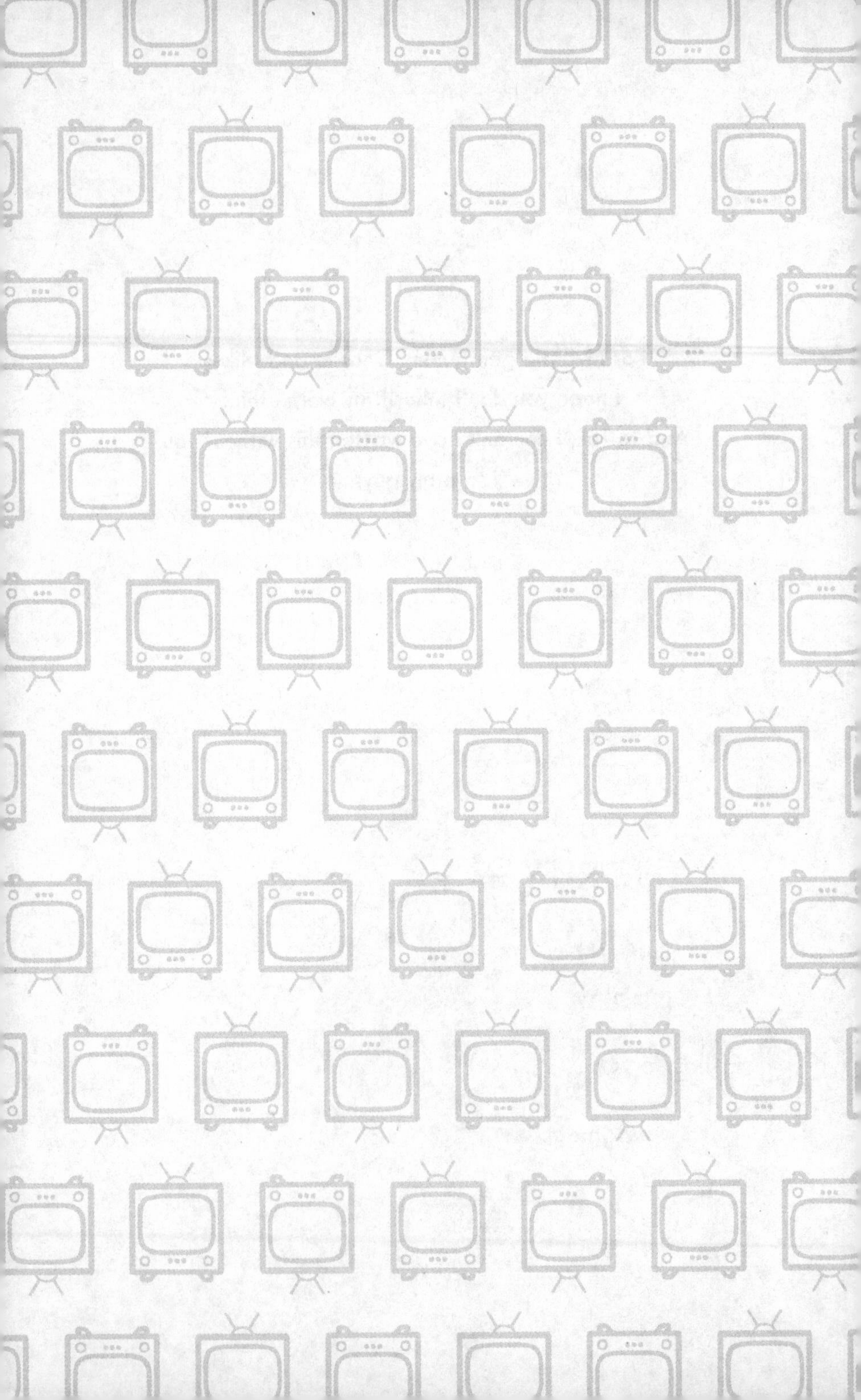

CONTENTS

THE **WORLD'S WORST** ASSISTANT

FOREWORD
BY CONAN O'BRIEN

It has long been accepted that what separates *Homo sapiens* from the rest of Earth's myriad creatures is our unending quest for perfection. Our constant need to improve our condition, from cave to hut to pyramid to castle to gilded manse to skyscraper, has pulled mankind from the swamps of ignorance and placed us, quite literally, atop the world. The Greeks, in their wisdom, defined "excellence" with the concept of Arete, a state of being in which one uses all of their mortal strength, bravery, and wit to achieve greatness. In Greek mythology, Arete is a great goddess, sheathed in brilliant white, who leads us higher, always higher, in our quest for ultimate perfection in our labors.

Enter Sona Movsesian. Sona, my assistant of thirteen years, believes that the pursuit of the divine Greek state of Arete is "lame" and should "go eat a dick." In fact, I only know about

Arete because when I asked Sona to assist me in researching her foreword, she told me to "stop being a bitch and find shit on Wikipedia." And so I did, and now we both know about this Arete lady. I was going to start this book with so much more research on the history of the work ethic and the Industrial Revolution, but when Sona and I join forces, I usually end up alone on Wikipedia while she uses my credit card to buy a jumbo bag of Doritos Locos Tacos Supreme. That, as many a youngster will tell you, is just "how we roll."

The title of this book, *The World's Worst Assistant*, may seem to many of you like a massive exaggeration—a cheap marketing ploy to grab eyeballs in an airport kiosk. But I assure you, the title of this book is shockingly apt. Sona, in many ways, is an absolutely awful personal assistant. By that I mean she isn't just bad or lazy, no—those words are far too inexact. Sona is actually quite brilliant and endlessly creative in her singular pursuit of her own comfort. I have always marveled at how hard the gangsters work in the movie *Goodfellas*, staying up weeks on end just to boost cheap cigarettes from a truck at LaGuardia. I eventually realized that these criminals worked much harder than most corporate CEOs because their very work was a declaration of their undying hatred for regulations and societal constraints. Sona, like any crime kingpin, is smart enough to play by the rules and win, but her deal with the devil has bound her to a life of lurid tricks, ingenious time-sucking distractions, and an unquenchable thirst to stick it to The Man. Believe me, I love it when people "stick it to The Man," it's just that sadly, in this tale, I am that Man.

Everything you are about to read is absolutely true and real. At times, you will shout aloud, "Just fire her, Conan! She's making a fool out of you!" But the truth is that Sona did not find her superpower as "World's Worst Assistant" until she met me in 2009. Criminologists believe that many a killing duo consists of two people who would never hurt a fly on their own. Leopold and Loeb, Bonnie and Clyde, the killing team in Capote's *In Cold Blood*—in all of these cases, two inert molecules join to form a deadly organism. Yes, Sona had the capacity to be "terrible," but she needed to find her killing partner, a boss so outrageous, childish, and nonsensical that together we could create an insane dynamic that few can believe. In an era where workplace professionalism is under a microscope, Sona and I are relentlessly and insistently idiotic. I give Sona the space to be Sona (see book), and she in turn gives me the space to knock a delicious cupcake out of her hand just as she is about to take a bite (to be clear, I am careful to strike the cupcake *only*, with great precision; and if you saw how much Sona wanted that delicious chocolate delicacy with whipped vanilla icing—you'd understand why I have no choice). Yes, the mess Sona and I have made of the modern workplace is a shared pursuit—we have forged these chains together—and if I were to fire her, she would immediately, and rightly, fire me.

At this point in my foreword it's safe to say that Sona has stopped reading and is searching her couch cushions for a gummy she lost last night while binge-watching *Too Hot to Handle*. In other words, I can now make one last point without Sona ever being the wiser, and that point is this: I trust

Sona with my life. She would do anything for me or my family, and she is one of the most honest and really caring people I know. She has been an unimaginably loyal friend during some very harrowing times, and I am lucky to have her at my side. I can even imagine that, one day, as I am lying on my deathbed and about to leave this world, it will be Sona who will be sitting by my side. "Sona . . . it's time . . . Go get my wife," I will gasp, barely able to speak. "Yes, Conan," Sona will say with great caring and empathy, as she pats my hand gently and says a silent prayer. "Rest easy, old boss, I'll get Liza right now."

Sona will then walk quietly out of my death chamber and soundlessly close the door. And, at that moment, she will completely forget what I asked her to do, pass my crying wife in the hallway, and head down the street to Forever 21, where she will shoplift a three-pack of hair scrunchies. I mean, someone is going to figure out I'm dead eventually and tell Liza I'm gone, so what's the big friggin' deal anyway?! And is Forever 21 really going to miss three suck-ass scrunchies?! Get the fuck off my back, brah!

This, dear reader, is the beautiful lesson Sona has taught me every single day.

CONAN O'BRIEN

Oxford, England

(Not really there, but it sounds cool)

INTRODUCTION

IT TAKES WORK TO BE THE WORLD'S WORST ASSISTANT.

It requires the same nerve and dedication as writing a book and asking your boss, a comedic icon and celebrated writer, to write the foreword and then following it up with drivel. If you bought this book specifically for the foreword, I don't blame you. I realize what a mistake it was to ask someone who was two-time president of the Harvard Lampoon, a writer on *Saturday Night Live*, a writer on *The Simpsons*, and a four-time Emmy winner to write the lead-in to this book. I have done none of those things, but the good news is I get paid for this book and he doesn't. So I win.

I take pride in knowing that my book has already peaked. I like that you assume the same—that way your expectations are low. This is a tactic I've used many times throughout my career as an executive assistant to Conan O'Brien . . . Keep the expectations *low*.

But it hasn't always been like this! I used to take pride in *reaching for high* expectations. So how did I get here? It's not as though you wake up one morning and think, "I'm just going to stop trying." It's a gradual process, and it's a process I know very well. I started strong: I worked long hours, sucked up when I needed to, and always went the extra mile. I strove to impress the people I worked for so I could move up. I wanted to start a career in television and thrive.

Then I got comfortable. The longer I stayed in my job, the more I thought, "This is good enough," and good enough turned into "This isn't what I saw for myself, but we'll roll with it," and that turned into "Well, I'm here."

This book will explore everything I learned on the path to becoming the World's Worst Assistant. My only hope is to pass down that wisdom to future generations of employees. Wondering how to watch a full feature-length film at work? I've got you covered. Thinking about taking a quick power nap at your desk? Let me show you how. More importantly, do you want to stop caring that your career isn't going as far as you thought it would? Then pull up a seat, pal.

In college, I would pull all-nighters and I graduated with honors from USC.

Last week, I left work for what I thought would be a quick errand and I was gone for three hours.

At NBC, I taught myself the basics of Photoshop so we could stop outsourcing press credentials for press conferences and parties to the graphics department, saving the publicity department money and solidifying my role on the team.

A month ago, I forgot to give Conan a copy of the monologue jokes for that day's show because I was stuck on the *New York Times* sudoku puzzle.

Marc Liepis, who at that time was the publicist for *Late Night with Conan O'Brien*, texted Conan right before my job interview with Conan and told him I was a rock star.

Last Monday, I failed to get a prescription refill of Conan's cholesterol medication because I was too busy binge-watching *Schitt's Creek* for the second time.

This book details the downfall of my ambition. What happened between college and now? How does someone who worked so hard to get her foot in the door end up as the World's Worst Assistant? Keep reading and I'll show you a brand-new world, one where deadlines are spurned, professionalism is seldom upheld, and you'll never have to miss an episode of your favorite TV show.

These are my memoirs, full of tips and guidelines on how to become me. What I lack in ambition and drive, I make up for in generosity. And now, by way of introduction . . .

Who Am I?

I'm Sona Movsesian. I have been working for Conan O'Brien since 2009, and I'm not great at my job.

TV was always an escape for me, albeit an escape from nothing. I grew up watching *Sesame Street*, *Mister Rogers*, and *Reading Rainbow*. I graduated to *Cheers* and both the TGIF programming on ABC and the Must See TV block on NBC.

My mother and I would watch *Beverly Hills, 90210* and *Melrose Place* together. I eventually made it to HBO, and from there, any dreams of a more "productive" hobby were over.

Buffy Summers got me. Jordan Catalano was the love of my life. Wayne Arnold reminded me of my brother.

I did a group project on HBO's TV model in my freshman speech class in college. In my sophomore creative writing class, I wrote an ode to the remote control.

When I was a junior in college, I told someone I wanted to work in television, and they told me I never would because I didn't have any connections. They weren't wrong about the connections, but I didn't believe that would stop me.

I went to a community college out of high school because I couldn't get into any of the schools I applied to. I had spent most of my high school years egging houses and not doing my homework. If you lived in Hacienda Heights, California, in the late '90s and woke up to find your home egged and didn't know who would do such a thing and didn't have any enemies to speak of, it was me and my friends. I'm sorry. You didn't deserve that. At the time, I didn't realize how destructive egging houses was. It's a thoughtlessness that I've tried to shake, but it has followed me throughout my life and still plagues me today. Act first, especially if it's funny; think later.

One day, my friends and I were spending the evening drawing hearts on the windshields of cars with whipped cream because it was close to Valentine's Day. We didn't realize there were two people in one of the cars. They followed us, pulled up next to us, and confronted us. What followed was a high-speed suburban car chase that resulted in almost $5,000 worth of damage to my friend Mikey's grandma's Cadillac. We eventually lost 'em by parking in someone's driveway, where we hid for about forty-five minutes until we felt like the coast was clear. That day we were scared straight and put our petty pranks behind us.

When I got to college, I excelled. I honestly don't know why I suddenly started to care about my grades after years of indifference. Transferring to a great school became a possibility.

I decided to enroll at the University of Southern California. That's where I saw a posting for an internship opportunity in the alternative programming department at NBC. I applied, interviewed, got the call offering me the internship, and went to Taco Bell to celebrate. This book seems as good a time as any to confess that I had no idea what the fuck "alternative programming" was when I applied. My twenty-year-old brain thought it was avant-garde filming until I learned (much longer into my internship than I'd like to admit) that the alternative programming department covers essentially any kind of entertainment programming that isn't episodic scripted television—TV movies, specials, variety specials, and reality programming. It was the first but not the last time I would successfully feign understanding in my career. Never ask questions and always pretend like you know what you're doing.

Speaking of pretending to know what you're talking about, I'd like to posit a scientific theory about working as an assistant in the entertainment industry (although this theory can be applied to working as an assistant in any industry, really).

The Human Centipede Theory

So what is this book? Am I the World's Worst Assistant because I'm terrible at my job, or do I hold that title because I chose to reject every preconceived notion of what it means to be someone's assistant?

We've seen so many images of Hollywood assistants being mistreated in their jobs—from the comical yet stress-inducing representations of getting lunch orders exactly right in *Set It Up* to the bleak and inhumane treatment depicted in *The Assistant*. But why? While some of these depictions may be exaggerated from the average assistant's experience, the sad reality is that many are true. There is a boss out there, right now, behaving as monstrously and abusively as the boss in *The Assistant*. Some poor assistant somewhere, right now, is being berated for a forgotten side order of French fries. When you're fresh out of college and ready to take on the world, it's amazing what behavior you'll allow well-functioning, professional adults to get away with.

When I had just graduated college, someone told me to work in an agency because they said that if I could get a year working at an agency under my belt, I could handle anything. I had heard stories of agents throwing printers at their assistants. Yelling was just a normal volume grown men and women decided (and still decide) to use while talking to their subordinates. I had always understood the appeal of working in the entertainment industry, even sacrificed a lot to do it, but if another human had ever thrown a printer at me, my earrings would have been coming off.

While thinking about this book and why some assistants allow themselves to be mistreated and, inversely, why some bosses in the industry love to mistreat, I was reminded of a movie I watched in the back of a tour bus with my friend Meghan in 2010 while on the Legally Prohibited from Being Funny on Television Tour: *The Human Centipede.*

The Human Centipede is a titillating tale of two women who encounter car trouble on the road and find themselves in the home of a terrifying man no normal human being would ever carry on a conversation with. From the moment he appears on the screen, he emits "creepy scientist" vibes. The women learn his plan is to unite them with another man he is holding captive by surgically connecting them ass to mouth, à la a human centipede.

But Sona, what does this have to do with the entertainment industry?

I'm getting to that.

In order to get nourishment, the person in the front of the centipede is allowed to eat normal food, and their bowel movements are unfortunately evacuated into the mouth of the person behind them, who has no choice but to gain nourishment from said bowel movements. They, in turn, evacuate their bowels into the third person in the centipede, who can then evacuate to the air. For the purpose of this theory, I am only sticking with the first installment of *The Human Centipede*, because the other two get a little out of hand, in my opinion.

Sona, I don't want to interrupt this incredibly disturbing retelling of this incredibly disturbing movie, but I'm just trying to figure out the point here.

I SAID I'M GETTING TO IT.

Okay, so what's the point of all this?

Well, my theory, which is based on no research and no scientific evidence and nothing really substantial, is that the hierarchy of the entertainment industry can be described as a metaphorical human centipede.

The people in the front (executives, agents, producers) consume. They turn that consumption into bile and excrement they inexplicably expel to the people beneath them. Those in the middle have no choice but to consume the excrement (the second step in the centipede), and they then expel to the people at the very end. Those people have no one to expel to, and thus, they just go into the bathroom stall and cry when no one is watching.

Sona, that's . . . still really disturbing. What happens when you get promoted?

You just move up in the centipede chain. You can now shit into someone else's mouth. And the shit you're eating is a little closer to the source. It's a cycle that doesn't end. Eat, shit, eat shit, get promoted, eat, shit in someone else's mouth, get promoted, eat good food, then inexplicably continue shitting in someone else's mouth because that's what you saw before you and it's all you know.

I've seen people mistreat others because they themselves were mistreated and think it's a rite of passage to treat someone like garbage. When you get to the top, you mix that with a tremendous amount of power and influence, and you feel like it gives you license to continue treating the people working below you poorly.

So how does the entertainment industry human centipede end? Easy. We can make the conscious decision not to treat other people we work with (interns, PAs, assistants) like they're literal trash.

I like to think the old guard is dying off. Conan started in the industry as one half of a legendary writing team with Greg Daniels. Conan never wanted to settle. He only ever wanted to work on shows he liked and believed in. For someone as smart and funny as Conan, that was actually possible. He was able to parlay his talent into respect early on in his career; ergo, no one ever shit in Conan's mouth (as far as I know). So when this loud, unruly woman walked into his life sixteen years after he began working as a late-night talk show host, he never felt the need to mistreat me. When I made mistakes, he never made me feel small. If he picked on me, he did so as an older brother, with endless teasing and an infuriating level of passive-aggressiveness, but never like he had the right to do it just because he was my boss.

So now the real reason I wanted to write a book explaining how to become a terrible assistant, per the norms. This is my advice to anyone looking to get into entertainment (or any field where bosses can get a little out of hand). Don't let someone shit in your mouth (of course I don't mean this literally—what you do in your private time is your business). Here are some pointers for how to deal with an unruly boss:

1. Lower their expectations. Is it 6 p.m., and are they asking you to get them a reservation at the hottest new restaurant in town for 7 p.m.? Did you try calling and the host laughed because it's impossible? Did you think about going to the restaurant and giving someone who had a 7 p.m. reservation money for their table? Did you think about going to the restaurant and talking to the manager directly and offering something like free tickets to a concert if they could make it work, even though you don't have free tickets to any concert and you would just stress yourself out more trying to get tickets to a concert that would seem appealing to someone you don't even know? Stop it. Don't do this. You can't get a reservation. Sometimes it can't be done. Tell them you tried and you couldn't make it happen. Then think of some other really great restaurants where you can easily make a reservation so they have some reasonable alternatives. If they look like they're about to shit in your mouth, close that mouth up. Not today, sir!

2. Say no. Are you being asked to fire an intern you like because they had the audacity to look at your boss in the face? If someone asks you to do something unreasonable, and especially something that is outside of your job description, it's okay to say no. On that same note, don't be afraid to ask for the things you need, including reasonable time off within the guidelines of your company's vacation policy. Don't miss Grandma's funeral because you have to go to your boss's house and organize his socks. Grandma deserves better. And you're allowed to miss a day of work.

3. Don't show them they're getting to you. If you have an extra-dicky boss who actually enjoys being at the head of the centipede, don't let them know they scare you. Because they shouldn't. I used to be intimidated by a few people at work. It's natural when you're just starting out. But the best skill I ever learned at work was how to openly tell someone if they're being rude to me. It's okay to stand up for yourself and it's okay to demand more from the people who you work for—you got the job because you're qualified and they don't want to spend the time training someone new, so chances are they're not going to fire you just because you stand up for yourself.

When I was thinking of what made me the World's Worst Assistant, the first thought that came into my head was that I'm not willing to compromise my emotional or physical well-being to get ahead. It's what we've seen from assistants in pop culture and in real life—the idea that we have to lose ourselves just so we can succeed in such a cutthroat business. I never did that. I once worked a stint in publicity assisting a couple stressed-out individuals, and they would take their stress out on me. I lasted two months before I realized it wasn't worth it, that taking the brunt of their unhappiness was only making me unhappy, and while I was doing fine at my job, my mental well-being and my job satisfaction were suffering. What I discovered in my time working for Conan was that I could abandon those preconceived ideas of what a traditional assistant is supposed to do and make the most of my position.

Is it possible this advice will get you fired? Unfortunately, yes. In an industry where bosses feel entitled to terrorize those who work for them, some won't take kindly to your refusal to eat shit. But is the mistreatment worth it? How much of your self-worth are you willing to give up in order to appease someone? What I'm saying is: you do not have to be the back of the centipede.

You can be the part of the centipede that breaks free. You can eat whatever you want and shit in a toilet. This analogy has run away from me, but what I'm trying to say is the mistreatment can end with you. This is a new generation of employees—all it takes is one person saying something bad about another person on Twitter, and that person can become a pariah. It's scary and it's beautiful. Let's rip our mouths from the asses of those who wish to oppress us and rise up! Everyone knows the assistants run Hollywood and NYC media anyway.

I, for one, love the change that's happening right now—not just in the entertainment industry but in all different industries. People are beginning to realize they don't have to be mistreated and get paid a small wage just to get ahead. We can live in a world where people treat others with respect and kindness and also get paid a livable wage. Harvey Weinstein is a monster and an abuser and now he's going to prison. Bill

O'Reilly screamed at people regularly and now he's no longer on the air. It's okay to be decent in a stressful business. If refusing to sew my mouth onto someone's ass makes me the World's Worst Assistant, then so be it.

Okay, no, wait. Actually, I have to be honest. I'm also sometimes very terrible at my job.

But I wasn't always terrible at my job. It's been quite the journey to get to this point.

Job History

By the time I graduated college, I had a résumé filled with an eclectic mix of past job experience and entertainment internships. What kind of impressive work experience does an assistant to one of the most beloved comedic minds have, you may ask? Let's take a look at the glamorous CV that landed me my dream job.

A Whopper of a Start to My Career

When I was sixteen, I got a job at the nearby Burger King during the summer between my junior and senior years. I wore a green shirt with black stripes, black pants, black shoes that looked orthopedic, and a visor. I don't know how any man resisted me. No photos exist of me in this ensemble. I started at the register, then felt a shocking sense of pride when they moved me to the drive-thru window. The drive-thru is not for the weak of heart—the goal is to collect the customer's money and get them their food within thirty seconds. I never felt such a sense of achievement as I did when I would look up at the clock and see that I had met that goal. I would look around to high-five someone, but no one was ever near me. They all acted as if the victory I had experienced was not a big deal. I wanted people to revel in my success, but since everyone was busy doing their jobs, I just reveled on my own. There were plenty of fist pumps and gentle murmurs of "You're killing it, Sones" under my breath.

So what were the takeaways? How did this work experience get me ready for my job as Conan's assistant? Was it learning to work under pressure, or perhaps to meet a tight deadline? Of course not. It was self-congratulation. When Conan is busy with his latest riff, especially one at my expense that gets everyone laughing at me, I go back to my desk, fist pump, and gently murmur, "You're killing it, Sones." In those moments when I looked for someone to celebrate my drive-thru victories with, I realized my favorite person to turn to for any validation or pats on the back is me. Does it help with my self-confidence? Not really. Is it sad? Yes, it is.

Moving on.

When I Learned to Nap at Work

During my senior year of high school and into my sophomore year of college, I worked at a watch store in the Puente Hills Mall called Tic Time. It was a mall job, which meant that it was dead during the week and picked up at night and during the weekend. More importantly, it also meant I got an employee discount at the food court. I ate teriyaki chicken bowls every day. Why not Genghis Khan Mongolian Grill, or perhaps the Great Steak & Potato Company, or Sbarro, or even Panda Express? Because the teriyaki-bowl place was right upstairs, and the rest of the food court was all the way on the other side of the mall. When I say my résumé was steeped in glamour and prepared me to work hand in hand with Hollywood's biggest stars, this is what I'm talking about.

At the watch store, my job was to greet customers and try to sell them the latest Fossil or Seiko models. If I was feeling particularly frisky, I would try to sell a Rado. I was told they make Rados with the same hard metal they use to make space shuttles. I don't know if it's true, but there was literally no lie I wouldn't tell in order to sell a watch. But it was a relatively quiet job. There were long periods in the day when no one would come in, and it was up to us to keep ourselves occupied. There were only so many times you could Windex the display cases, so I started reading. One summer, I started reading *Helter Skelter*, which, by the way, is the worst book for anyone working in retail to read. Nothing says "Buy a watch" like seeing the customer service representative reading a book about mass murders committed by a drugged-out '60s cult. Sometimes, when it was especially slow, I would lie down behind the counter and close my eyes and deeply relax.

Okay. Nap. I would nap.

Amid all the glamour, all the lying to customers and scaring them with my choice of book, my stint at Tic Time can be boiled down to a single moment—a simple moment. A couple came in to change a watch battery.

Occasionally someone would come in to change a battery. It's supposedly an easy job, but for some reason it terrified me. If a battery was easy to change, we would just do it in the shop. If it had a tricky battery backing or an intricate glass on the face, we would have to take down their info and send it somewhere to get it fixed. I don't know where. The watch disappeared one day and then just showed up again the next. It was also entirely possible that someone who knew how to change batteries would just come in and do them. I never paid attention to anything that was going on around me. Anyway, this couple came in and asked me to change a battery and it had an intricate glass on the face, but for some reason that day I thought, "Eh, what the hell," and I tried to do it myself. When I put it on the contraption that sealed the battery backing back on the watch, the beautiful intricate glass just shattered.

I stood there thinking of things I could say to cover up what I had just done. I began to panic and almost started to cry, right there in the Tic Time. I thought of excuses where the watch was blamed. Could I blame the couple? No, but I thought of ways to blame them. I stood there for what felt like hours but was only minutes, staring at this watch with a now shattered glass and thinking of things I could say that could divert the blame from me. I walked over to them and said:

"I'm so sorry. When I put your watch in the contraption to seal the backing, I smashed the glass. I feel terrible. We will cover the cost of the repair, and I'll be sure to tell my manager what I did."

And they shrugged, smiled, and said, "That's okay, it happens."

Who the fuck were these people? No anger, no frustration, just complete understanding. Is honesty really the way to approach anything that goes wrong, or were these people just sick? This day clearly left me with a lot to consider.

After that episode, every time I did something wrong at work, I told the truth about it like some sick fuck. Just pure, unadulterated honesty. It's gotten to the point where even if I'm not involved in something that goes wrong but have some peripheral connection to it, I will apologize and take responsibility. Surprisingly, this became more of an enormous asset as I started setting the bar lower and lower at work. How do you stay angry at someone who acknowledges their mistakes and apologizes? You can't. If there's one part of my job that I'm actually good at, it's recognizing my shortcomings.

When I Almost Started to Mature . . .

While in college, I took on a few different jobs. The first was as a peer tutor. One of the people I tutored was a football player for the college, and I distinctly remember him trying to convince me that the contraction "won't" does not have an apostrophe in it. He was beautiful, though, so I didn't care. And those arms. Who cares about apostrophes when you have arms like that? The only thing I really learned from this job was where to put commas and that I would let handsome men get away with bad grammar. Also that maybe I wasn't cut out to be a tutor . . .

I moved on to other student jobs while I was at USC. I

had qualified for work-study through the financial aid program and got a gig at the College of Letters, Arts and Sciences public relations department. I loved this job and it was the first time I got a raise. I worked there for two semesters and actually did the work I was assigned to do. It felt like personal growth, maybe because it was.

. . . Until I Got Fired from a Los Angeles Landmark

The next glamorous stop on my way to becoming a very fancy television assistant was working at the Hollywood Bowl. When I applied to work at the Hollywood Bowl, I had an image in my mind where I would do my job, then stand discreetly in the background watching all the shows at the Bowl. That is not what happened.

I worked at one of the four stores that were on the property with volunteers who were typically retired seniors. They were always such kind, lovely people. Then, when the show would start, these asshole volunteers would take their aprons off and sprint to the Bowl to watch the show, leaving me, the paid employee, to sit and rot in the merch store, waiting for someone to leave the show to shop. I never had such FOMO in my life. I had never been so jealous of old people.

I would always get an afternoon shift, which started around 2 p.m. and would normally end around 11 p.m., so there was never any time to do anything afterward. Try to put yourself in my shoes for a second: you're completely bound to the Hollywood Bowl with no time to go to the beach or the movies or just enjoy time with that guy you really liked who didn't give you much of a hint of whether he felt the same way but loved going to get burgers with you and you interpreted that to mean he liked you because you would talk literally all the time but then anytime there was a moment where he could make a move he wouldn't because maybe he was super shy but at that point he didn't need to be because you made it more than obvious that you were completely open to the two of you moving on to a different phase in your relationship and you would stay up late at night wondering if you should just make a move but then you got scared because you kept picturing yourself making a move and him rejecting you and you realized there was no way your ego would ever recover from that so you did nothing.

Anyway, what was I talking about? Oh yeah, the Hollywood Bowl. In July, I got some friends tickets to see Röyksopp, Basement Jaxx, and Bossacucanova. From my distant perch at the merch shop, I could tell it was the loudest and most exciting concert I'd ever heard. I could see beams of colored lasers shooting out and smoke billowing beyond the very tall walls that were blocking my view of what was apparently the greatest concert of the season. I heard people squealing with pure joy, and everyone who went to the bathroom jogged out and back into the Bowl with the greatest look of happiness on their faces, like they had just witnessed an electronic music miracle that would only happen once in a lifetime.

There's nothing like sitting in a tiny store alone listening to 17,000 people having the time of their lives. To add insult to injury, one of our managers walked out, sweaty and out of breath with a giant smile beaming over his face, like he had just gone to the best rave of his life, and said, "It's INSANE in there!" He then told me that for the first time in the years he had been working at the Hollywood Bowl, the residents in the houses nearby in the Hills were calling and complaining about the noise.

To be so close yet so far to a concert like this was akin to torture for me. I couldn't go through that again.

I had already told the managers that I had planned a trip with my cousins to go to Australia during August, so I asked management what I should do about it—taking two weeks off during a seasonal job is a hefty request, so I thought they'd just tell me not to come back, but they didn't. I wanted the trip to be my excuse to leave and enjoy whatever was left of my summer, but they told me they would hold my job for me until I got back. Goddammit.

When I got back from Australia, however, I was completely over the idea of summer work. I needed my summer and I needed my freedom, but they had held my job for me and I couldn't just quit now. And so I did what I thought was less of a terrible move and just stopped showing up after a couple weeks. I thought it would make me an awful person to quit flat out. What would I even say? It's similar to when you're dating someone and you don't want to break up with them because it's too hard and involves awkward confrontation, so you just start becoming a terrible partner hoping they'll wise up and dump you. I wanted the Hollywood Bowl to dump me because I was too immature and dumb.

Labor Day was one of their busiest weekends, and my friends were planning a trip to Palm Springs. What a perfect time to piss off my incredibly understanding and lovely bosses and do THEM the favor of giving them the perfect opportunity to fire me. I called in with a lame excuse on Friday, then again on Saturday, and finally on Sunday they called me and said they wouldn't need my services anymore. You're welcome, Hollywood Bowl! You held my job for me for two weeks during a very limited season, and I repaid you with terrible work ethic and complete lack of communication.

What did I learn from this ordeal that has carried on to working for Conan?

Um, nothing. Show up to work? Don't set your desk up mere feet away from an iconic arena and expect to get anything done? Most importantly, I guess, don't be an asshole. For years I justified what I did by chalking it up to youth, but while writing this book, I texted my cousins to ask when we went to Australia, and it turns out I wasn't an immature teenager but in my early twenties, which changed the narrative from me being young and stupid to being old enough to know better. There is no excuse for what I did, and I think about it every time I go to the Hollywood Bowl and I see that poor sad sap of a seasonal worker sitting in a small store watching everyone walk into the venue to witness a memorable show.

I waited a few years before I told Conan about the time I got fired from the Hollywood Bowl. He was understandably horrified, yet amused.

My First Postcollege Job

After I graduated from college, I worked for an entertainment research company. It sounded impressive when I told people, but it couldn't have been further from what I was interested in pursuing. How did I end up in a research job I didn't want? Maybe because when asked—since I didn't know what I wanted to pursue—I would shrug and say, "Research?"

I commuted for two hours and worked in an office with people I had nothing in common with. After about three days, I wanted out. After another week and a half, I walked into my boss's office first thing and told her it just wasn't working. At lunchtime that same day, I got a call from the Page Program at NBC saying I had gotten accepted into the program. I had interviewed six months earlier, so I had honestly just forgotten about it until they called me.

There is nothing I learned from the entertainment research job. I wasn't there long enough to learn more than where they kept their office supplies.

When Everything Clicked

I loved being an NBC page. I got a firsthand glimpse into how television shows were developed. Since I didn't know exactly what I wanted to do, it was perfect for me. The only thing I didn't like about it was the uniform. As a page, I wore nearly the exact same outfit Kenneth the Page wore on *30 Rock*—a white button-down shirt, a blue polyester blazer, and a tie with a peacock print. The only difference was mine included an ill-fitting gray skirt with black tights. It was as bad as you're imagining.

I hated that uniform.

For six weeks, I wore it to give tours. We trained for the tour by following other pages giving tours, and I have to admit that so much of the information I imparted when giving my own tours was incorrect or made up. Some of the lies were like jokes passed down through generations of pages. Others were my own original material. If you took a tour of the NBC Burbank lot in 2006 from a girl who had curly hair and was wearing a disheveled uniform, most of the information you received was not true. No, the architecture at the NBC building in Burbank was not constructed so other networks wouldn't be able to look through the windows and spy on their ideas. And no, Johnny Carson didn't have a tanning bed in his dressing room that he used before every show. Ninety percent of what I said was fabricated. Sorry about that.

Anyway, the tours I gave were of the NBC Burbank lot, an aesthetically displeasing lot, but it was home to sets that tours always wanted to see. Sets for shows such as *Days of Our Lives*, *Access Hollywood*, and *The Tonight Show with Jay Leno*. That's it. That was the tour. We weren't allowed to go into the actual set for *Days of Our Lives* because tourists kept stealing props, so we would stand outside the stage door, behind a yellow line, peering into a nondescript set mostly blocked by large wooden walls, and say, "And this is the set for *Days of Our Lives*!" The people in my tour would crane their necks to peek inside. We would stand there for about three minutes, and then move on. If you were one of the unfortunate individuals who took the tour later in the afternoon, both the *Access Hollywood* and *Tonight Show with Jay Leno* sets would be closed due to filming, so the exterior walls of the *Days of Our Lives* set would be all you would see. Not exactly the thrill of a lifetime.

I used to feel bad about it, but on one of my tours, Bryan Dattilo, who plays Lucas Horton on *Days of Our Lives*, happened to be outside of the studio, and two of the women on my tour LOST IT. They almost started crying. Dattilo was very lovely and agreed to take a photo with them and spoke to them for a bit and even complimented one on her perfume. I've never seen two women so excited in my life. When he went back to filming, the one he had complimented shrieked in her Southern accent, "I'm never going to stop wearing my White Diamonds perfume!"

Everyone else in the tour was thrilled for them, especially me. I was so cynical about these tours coming to see what I thought were lame sets that I hadn't realized that people all over the country watched these shows daily—maybe they had for years—and were thrilled to be anywhere in the orbit of where their favorite programs were made. I eventually found out that these two women had flown to LA specifically to see where *Days of Our Lives* was filmed, and they couldn't care less that all they saw were these massive wooden walls. They knew what was beyond those walls, and being so close to it all was enough for them.

While I was in the Page Program, I was assigned to the events and operations coordinator in the publicity department. I worked on premiere parties, wrap parties, and tons of other press events. I hustled. It led to a permanent job in the department, and I loved it there. The seedlings of my future deteriorated work ethic for Conan would be planted at this job—although I was good at being a coordinator, I would sneak in breaks to watch *Jerry Springer* at a high volume on the television in the communal area. There, of course, were other signs that I was taking a more relaxed approach to my work.

Some of the Signs

I would have to say the biggest turning point in my career was when I was the events and operations coordinator at NBC. It's where I really worked my networking chops, and it's what gave me the connections I needed to ultimately get the job I'm in now. It's also where my confidence translated into a more relaxed approach to my job. The more I worked there, the more comfortable I got. The more comfortable I got, the more I allowed more of myself to seep into my job. Once I began to do that and really feel as though I was getting acceptance rather than repulsion, I acknowledged that this was the approach I was going to take throughout my career, no matter the position. Of course, as my drive to be perfect decreased over time, things started to fall through the cracks. And you know what? I was okay with that.

When I was the events and operations coordinator, my job was to keep track of RSVPs for various events like press conferences, wrap parties, premiere parties, etc. I would check the RSVP line or email, then make a note of whether a guest was attending an event or politely declining. This is something I needed a college degree to do, apparently.

One of the events I worked on was the luncheon after Dick Wolf's Hollywood Walk of Fame star ceremony in March of 2007. His star was right outside the Hollywood Roosevelt Hotel on Hollywood Boulevard, which was where his luncheon would be held. The guest list included many of television's power players—producers, executives, and stars from his illustrious shows like *Law & Order* and all the other *Law & Order*s.

My job at this luncheon was to stand at the door leading into the restaurant with my trusty clipboard and the RSVP list I had spent hours attending to. I had pored over that list so many times that if you told me your name, I wouldn't even have to check the list; I would just know whether you were on it from memory. And yet, as I discovered very early on in my tenure as the events and operations coordinator, the carefully maintained and memorized list would become completely meaningless to me as soon as the doors opened.

If you tried to come to an NBC event and I was working at the door, you would be let into the party. It didn't matter if you were on the list, because even if I knew you weren't on the list, I would be so terrified that you were an executive or someone's dad that I didn't have the balls to turn you away. You know those people at clubs with their clipboards and pouty faces who happily reject you if you aren't on the list? I'm not those people. I think that if you made the effort to dress up and drive all the way to Spago or the Beverly Hilton or the Ritz in Pasadena, then you deserve to be inside the party. I considered this using my powers for good.

Usually this benevolence caused no issue. No one ever noticed a few random faces in the crowd—that is, until the Dick Wolf Hollywood Walk of Fame luncheon. On the same day as the luncheon, there was another event being held in a different room of the Roosevelt Hotel that also had quite a few men: the welcome reception for the seventh annual Playboy Golf Scramble Championship. It was a lovely outdoor event where golfers could mingle with Playboy Playmates. While I was working the door at Dick Wolf's luncheon, their event ended and I saw many skinny and beautiful and incredibly scantily clad women coming up to me and asking if they could come in. I knew they weren't supposed to be there. But Playboy Playmates wanted to check out Dick Wolf's luncheon at this steak restaurant. Maybe they were hungry? Or bored? Either way, they were nice to me, so I let them all in. Was it the right thing to do? Of course not—my job was specifically to keep uninvited people out. They weren't on the list. What's the point of the list if I was just going to ignore it? So why did I do it? I thought it would be funny to tell my friends later.

"Hey, how was work today?"

"It was really cool. Dick Wolf got a star on the Hollywood Walk of Fame and had a luncheon at the steak restaurant in the Roosevelt right after. I worked the door."

"That sounds fun."

"That part was neat, but the best part was when I let a bunch of Playboy Playmates into his party."

"What?"

And so on.

At one point, I looked in the restaurant and saw groups of men and leggy, thin, and beautiful women mingling with one another. The event was a sea of well-dressed media professionals in suits, skirts, and blazers alongside a sprinkling of women in six-inch heels, incredibly short skirts, and shirts that aggressively showed off their assets.

The women became so noticeable that our head of security came up to me and asked what was happening. I had done it—I had finally allowed so many interlopers into one of our parties that the jig was up. How could I tell our head of security that I thought it would be funny if these Playboy Playmates rolled into Dick Wolf's luncheon? How could I tell him I never checked the list I spent weeks putting together? How could I tell him my need to be liked and lack of confidence had kept me from turning people away at the door, and all someone had to do was be nice to me and I'd gladly lift the velvet rope for them and their friends despite whatever relationship they might or might not have to the event? I decided I couldn't, and told him they must have slipped in through a side door.

Our head of security had to go to each woman and politely ask her to leave Dick Wolf's luncheon.

✦

At another event, I was asked to put the playlist together for a daytime party that Jeff Zucker, the then head of NBC, would be throwing. Zucker had wanted the song "Bartender" by an artist named Rehab on the playlist. I didn't tell anyone at the time, but in the days before subscription streaming services, I would download the songs off LimeWire, viruses and all, and put them on my iPod. I downloaded the uncensored version for reasons I still don't understand, and the chorus of the song went like this:

So I jacked the keys to her fuckin' car
Crashed that piece of shit and then stepped away

This played at a daytime party with the highest brass of NBCUniversal in attendance. What's worse is I only put four songs on the playlist, so this would play every twenty minutes or so. Each time it played, I would see people look up confused, breaking whatever important conversation they were clearly having and trying to understand why such an inappropriate song would be playing at such an important event. Eventually I stopped being embarrassed and started to be amused.

Despite all my very obvious shortcomings, my bosses in the events department liked me. Instead of reprimanding me, they flew me to New York the following year to be in charge of a list of roughly eight hundred people for the premiere party of Candace

Bushnell's new show *Lipstick Jungle* at Saks Fifth Avenue. It turned out my typical laid-back approach would not be appreciated there. The only time anyone truly yelled at me was during this party's preparation. Candace Bushnell would call my line and leave a voicemail with names to add to this massive list for the party. Then, shortly after, she would ask for a copy of the updated list for her review. One time I sent it without checking my messages, and the most recent names she wanted to add weren't there. She was not happy. She called me and reprimanded me for not doing my job, so I deployed my tried-and-true tactic of apologizing and telling her it was my mistake and it wouldn't happen again. To my shock and horror, she didn't care. If I were her assistant instead of Conan's, I would not be writing this book. My instinct was to calm her down by telling her that whoever came to Saks Fifth Avenue would be let in, but I quickly realized that was definitely not the response she wanted to hear.

Anyway, by the time the party actually happened, I did actually let in anyone who came to the door and the party went off without a hitch. I doubt anyone who was affiliated with the show or Candace Bushnell knew anyone at that party. But hey, that's showbiz, baby.

How I Got My Job

Like a lot of people my age, I always considered Conan O'Brien my late-night host. I didn't have a dog in the fight when it came to whether Jay Leno or David Letterman was better, but at 12:35 a.m., I was always watching *Late Night with Conan O'Brien*. It was a treat when my parents let my brother and me stay up to watch. We spent hours laughing in the glowing light, perhaps sacrificing our alertness at school the next day for Conan's sake.

People often talk about their favorite *Late Night* sketches, but personally, I loved the monologues. Conan jumped around and popped out of frame and did a dance where he pretended strings were attached to his hips.

When I heard Conan would be hosting *The Tonight Show* from Los Angeles, I talked to HR about getting a job on his new show. I remember being overly confident about my odds. I decided I wanted to move from working at the network to production, and anytime anyone asked what I would be doing after my time in the publicity department, I would say, "I'm going to work for Conan O'Brien." I don't know where that confidence came from, but it was almost like I manifested my career.

A few months after I spoke with HR, I applied to an online posting for a job on Conan's *Tonight Show*, and my résumé was put into a pile for prospective applicants to be Conan's assistant. I interviewed with the line producer, Sarah Federowicz. I had my second interview the next day with Sarah, the producer Tracy King, and Conan himself.

The interview was being held in someone's office, and when I walked in, it was all I could do to hide how starstruck I really was. This was the *Days of Our Lives* set, and I was the woman with White Diamonds perfume. I was wearing purple (my power color) and trying to concentrate, but the whole time I was there I was thinking, "Holy shit, I'm interviewing to be Conan O'Brien's assistant."

When I first walked into the interview, I met Tracy, then Sarah, and finally Conan introduced himself and told me to be as comfortable as I'd like and that the interview wouldn't be formal. I said, "Is it okay if I lie down on the couch?" The three of them laughed, and later that same day, I got a call from HR that I had gotten the job. The HR rep told me that Conan liked my couch joke. I got my job working for Conan because I made a joke about being lazy—foreshadowing at its best.

Very quickly into my tenure of being Conan's assistant, my being starstruck dissipated, and eventually this comedic icon whom I had admired my entire adolescent life became . . . a nuisance. It was almost as if I put more effort into *getting* my job than I did at *working* in my job. I felt so much ambition and did everything I could to get hired, and as soon as I realized what a fun environment I would be working in, that ambition slowly began to fade. Conan became this guy who would make me high-five him after he made fun of me. He told people I stole babies from the marketplace in my spare time for fun. He said my dad carved my brother out of wood just because my dad has a mustache. He smacks food out of my hand when I'm eating and laughs in my face while I pick the food up off the floor. Despite both his and my juvenile tendencies, I know that after everything I've done to get to this point, I'm exactly where I'm supposed to be and working for the person I'm meant to be working for. But maybe I'm getting ahead of myself. Let me tell you about some of my early misadventures as Conan's right-hand woman.

PART ONE

In The Devil Wears Prada, *Anne Hathaway's character, Andrea, angers Meryl Streep's character, Miranda Priestly, so Miranda orders Andrea to get her the unpublished manuscript of the new Harry Potter book. What follows is a spiral many assistants have gone through—the feeling that completing an important task is impossible and not completing it will cost you your job. At the last minute, after exhausting every possible option, Andrea's writer acquaintance finds a way to get the impossible manuscript, and Andrea proves her worth to Miranda. I think about this scene a lot. The sheer panic Andrea exhibits as she calls every publisher contact she has while fetching Miranda's lunch, running various other errands, and completing her daily tasks . . . the total dread in realizing she won't be able to accomplish the task and therefore will fail at this job she really wants to excel in . . . and finally the euphoria in successfully accomplishing the task and smugly telling Miranda she crushed it. When I think about this scene, I realize that I have never felt any of these things. Over the course of this book, we'll consider how the scene might play out if the interaction involved me and Conan instead of Anne and Meryl.*

CONAN: Sona!

No answer.

CONAN: SONA!

David, Sona's office mate, hears Conan calling for Sona. He looks over, and Sona has her earphones in and is laughing at her computer screen. He calls her. Sona sees David's name blinking on the phone and answers, even though he's only twenty feet away and they can comfortably speak to each other.

SONA: David?

DAVID: He's calling you.

Sona hangs up and enters Conan's office.

SONA: Sorry, I was doing some filing and got caught up.

CONAN: I need the new Robert Caro book to read on my trip.

SONA: Okay, I'll send Brad to Barnes & Noble.

CONAN: Did you fall and smack your little head on the pavement?

SONA: No one has ever said my head is little.

CONAN: I have all the published Robert Caro books. I need to know what happens in the new one.

SONA: Can't you just wait until it comes out?

CONAN: I want it now.

SONA: Okay, so you want the unpublished manuscript for the new Robert Caro historical nonfiction?

CONAN: I've been on television forever. It shouldn't be hard.

SONA: You didn't say please.

CONAN: Are you serious?

SONA: This is a big ask. It would be nice to hear a please.

Conan rolls his eyes and reluctantly mumbles, "Please."

SONA: Was that hard? Why is it hard to say please?

CONAN: So tell me again what you're going to do.

SONA: I hate when you pop-quiz me after you ask me to do something like I'll forget right away.

CONAN: I didn't see you write it down.

SONA: I don't need to write it down. It's easy to remember.

CONAN: Okay, just tell me what I asked you to do, then.

SONA: No, it's insulting. I have to go do it anyway.

Sona returns to her desk. She lied—she did, in fact, forget what Conan asked her to do immediately after he asked it—but she doesn't want to tell him because then he'll be smug about it and it'll infuriate her. She sits at her desk and puts her earphones back in . . . It'll come to her eventually.

EFFORT

IN THIS CHAPTER WE'RE GOING TO EXPLORE THE IDEA OF "EF-fort." What you put into your job can dictate how much you get out of it. So what happens when you put in just enough, but not too much?

When I was first hired, Conan was still in New York in his final season of *Late Night with Conan O'Brien*. I started working for him in the beginning of January of 2009, but he wouldn't wrap up the show until February. He eventually moved to California in March of that year, and I spent my first three months as his assistant working remotely. I remember finding an empty office at NBC and taking meticulous notes for the ways I could help him and his family transition their lives from New York to California.

The day after I got word that I'd be working for Conan, I met him at a Peet's Coffee in Brentwood with a booklet about Los Angeles that I made myself and a notepad to take notes.

I handed the booklet to Conan at our meeting—a lifelong Angeleno handing over all her knowledge to the new kid in town. It was so important to me to make a good impression that I'd spent all day fastidiously putting together essential information about Los Angeles, and then took it to Kinko's to get it laminated and bound. Conan had lived in Los Angeles sixteen years prior, but I thought it would be good to show him how I would go the extra mile.

During our coffee meeting, I remember telling Conan that I wanted to work on something that inspired me and that I was proud to be a part of. His humility and decency were what really struck me. Right after I left, I met up with my brother and sister-in-law at a restaurant in Toluca Lake, and I was noticeably shaken. I'd known that taking this job would change my life forever, but I hadn't realized how nice of a person Conan would be. That first meeting made me want to work harder for him.

A couple days after I got the job, Conan's wife, Liza, wrote me the nicest email introducing herself and telling me a little about their family and sent me a photo of their kids, Neve and Beckett, who at the time were five and three. I have to admit that before I got to know Conan and his lovely wife a little better, I had been most worried about Liza. Was she going to be a trophy wife who would abuse me or be stereotypically awful? Was she going to yell at me if I forgot to tell her about a change in Conan's travel itinerary? Would I be asked to pick up her dry cleaning in the middle of a workday? What I learned very quickly was that Liza is not only brilliant and kind and decent, but also my most important ally. She became a sounding board whenever I felt like I was having a tough time with Conan. I often say that my favorite thing about Conan is Liza, and that is a sentiment that only gets truer as time goes on.

So why am I saying all this sappy stuff? Because when I first got my job, I *wanted* to do the best I could. I needed to make sure that this very nice man and his wonderful wife were happy. I was now a part of their lives. Assistants get close to the people they work for, and I knew that over time, the O'Briens would become very important figures in my life. I was right about that.

Reminiscing about those early days—back in a time when I enthusiastically went to Kinko's to bind and laminate a homemade booklet in hopes of being helpful—it's hard to say when my relationship with Conan went from being professional to the dysfunctional mess it is now.

It could've been when, three months into my job, I was speaking Armenian on the phone with my grandmother and Conan asked if I was arguing with Dracula.

It also could've been a year later, when he told *Rolling Stone* magazine that I floated to this country in a basket while my father was in the midst of a goat attack on the island of Armenia (I was born in Los Angeles, my father is not a goat herder, and Armenia is landlocked).

All I know is that something happened, or gradually happened, to make me go from the girl who makes booklets to the girl who occasionally slips a marijuana edible into her lunch.

Conan became the second older brother I never wanted. The dynamic shifted, and so did my work ethic.

I'm happy to take most of the blame for my gradual decline in any willingness to work. But doesn't my boss deserve some credit? Wouldn't the World's Worst Assistant need to be enabled by the World's Worst Boss?

Neve and Beckett used to always say that Conan melted half my brain. When asked what happened to the other half, they would say that other half was already melted before I met him. I have never heard a better description of me.

Am I proud of what I've become? Yes. I get paid to do the bare minimum. Is this where I saw myself? No. But then again, everything I've been fortunate enough to experience has been a pleasant surprise. Would I try harder at another job? Yes, without a doubt. So when Conan retires, please hire me. Until then, I will proudly take my place on the Mount Rushmore of terrible assistants . . . alone. I know there are other bad assistants out there—I'm sure of it—but I refuse to share my title as the worst in the world.

The One When I Binged *Friends*

We all have heroes.

In 2009, a young boy from Singapore named Joseph Schooling met his hero Michael Phelps. Seven years later, Schooling would beat Phelps at the 2016 Rio Olympics in the 100-meter butterfly.

Naomi Osaka grew up in Long Island, New York, idolizing Serena Williams. At twenty, she would compete against Williams in the US Open and win.

When I heard Robert De Niro was suing his former assistant for, among many other things, watching fifty-five episodes of *Friends* in four days while at work, I can only imagine I felt the same thing Schooling and Osaka felt when they first saw their heroes excel . . . Fifty-five episodes? In four days? While at work? I had never been so in awe of anyone. A small piece of me thought, "Fifty-five episodes? I could do better than that."

Luckily, one of our writers thought that it was an excellent idea that I should devote my week to beating De Niro's assistant's record.

Each episode of *Friends* is about twenty-two to twenty-three minutes long. To watch fifty-five episodes, you'd have to allot 1,265 minutes of your life, or a little over twenty-one hours. To watch fifty-five episodes, you'd have to watch about 5.5 hours of *Friends* per day for four days straight. To make things even more difficult, my workday starts at 10 a.m., and I would have until we taped at 4:30 p.m. to watch as many episodes as possible. That's 6.5 hours of time I had to watch 5.5 hours of TV just to keep up with De Niro's assistant. I cracked my knuckles and got to work.

For four days, I binged. I laughed. I cried. I started forcing my friends to meet me in coffee shops. I would move sofas with unwilling pals just so I could yell "Pivot!" I stopped giving the middle finger and started pounding my fists together. I became the living embodiment of *Friends*. At the end of the four-day timeline, I had watched fifty-eight episodes. Like a motherfucking champion.

As a gift from Conan for beating De Niro's assistant's

record, I got all fifty-eight episodes I watched on VHS, a basket full of marijuana edibles, and six puppies named after each of the main characters on *Friends*.

I guess I should rewind a bit and explain how I became so brazen about watching TV at work.

When I first started interning at NBC, I noticed that everybody who worked there had a TV either at their desk or in their office. When working in television, wouldn't it make sense to have a television at your disposal? It's there to watch the shows you're working on—to watch edits of various episodes and keep up with the content you're distributing globally. It's also to keep up with whatever is going on in the world. Is someone from a show you're working on stopping by *The View*? Then you should watch the interview on your TV. Is *Extra* going to do a special segment on the show you're adapting from a popular novel? Then here's your TV to stay in the know.

Somewhere down the line, I noticed no one ever cared what you were watching. It's not like they could keep up with how every show was being promoted, and they could never say something you were watching wasn't pertinent to your job because no one ever really knew, so I made it a habit to have the TV on all the time. When I was the events and operations coordinator, my desk was in the common area in the middle of all these offices, and the TV I watched was affixed to the wall. That's when I learned I could watch *Jerry Springer* every day at a very high volume. I can't imagine how annoying it was to everyone I worked with, and I'm shocked no one ever said anything about it. I do remember a lot of the office doors remained closed throughout the entire day, and now I wonder if my regularly scheduled programming might have had something to do with it. Regardless, passively watching television for work eventually became just watching television because it's there. And that's how they thought of me for this segment—through my brazen and widely known disregard for office etiquette and my unapologetic attitude toward watching TV at work.

Anyway, the day after I beat the *Friends* binging record, I forced Jeff Ross's assistant, David Hopping, to come with me to all the locations on the Warner Bros. lot where they shot *Friends*.

The following week, I took all the photos and footage I shot visiting the locations on the lot and edited a movie in iMovie with the *Friends* theme as the background music. I uploaded it to Instagram, but it was taken down within five minutes because of copyright infringement. The locations were fine, but I couldn't use the theme song. So I enlisted David again, this time asking him to drop everything he was doing so we could figure out a way to get around the copyright infringement issues with the theme song. I decided the best thing to do would be to sing it myself with David as the backup (the "clapper").

How much time did I waste? We already know that from Monday to Thursday, I watched almost twenty-three hours of television. We spent about five hours on Friday going to all the locations on the Warner Bros. lot. I spent another two hours editing the video and another hour dealing with the *Friends* copyright infringement debacle on Instagram. All in all, I calculate thirty-one hours of my workweek were completely wasted on this *Friends* binge challenge. Additionally, if you factor in the breaks I take for the bathroom and lunch and doing the crossword puzzle and socializing, then I'm actually in overtime. I got paid my regular work salary, plus overtime, plus appearance fees for the show, so I made a nice profit from watching TV at work and doing no real work. Plus, I stole David away for a few hours to help me with the photo shoot and Instagram post.

I don't have any Olympic medals, and I've never won a Grand Slam title, but I'm sure whatever Schooling and Osaka felt when they beat their idols is a fraction of the joy I felt when I beat Robert De Niro's former assistant's binging record. Like her, I was fortunate enough to find my purpose and excel at my goals. Like her, I will be remembered forever. This is my legacy.

My Journal During the Tour

During the Legally Prohibited from Being Funny on Television Tour, I kept a journal. I should rephrase that: for less than the first half of the Legally Prohibited from Being Funny on Television Tour, I kept a journal. After our show in San Jose on May 5, I just stopped. Why? Because I was either eating or drinking and forgot. My unfinished journal is a perfect representation of how I approach things both at work and in my personal

HOW TO WATCH TV AT WORK

1: Wait until your boss has left the general vicinity.

2: Make sure your screen is not visible from your boss's office.

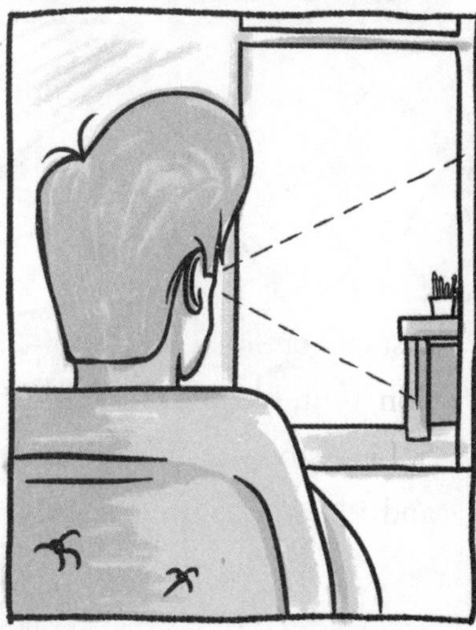

WATCH TV (cont.)

3: Put in one headphone, not both. That way you can still hear your boss if he needs something.

4: Only wear two headphones if it's worth it (e.g., I did it for the Red Wedding episode of *Game of Thrones*).

5: Watch something. Be sure to have actual work files open behind whatever you're watching so you can minimize the window quickly and look like you've been working all along.

WATCH TV (cont.)

6: Make sure whatever you're watching is appropriate. You wouldn't want to disrespect your workplace... Also, if you get caught, it could be an HR issue.

7: Try to minimize your facial reactions so others don't notice you're watching TV.

8: If someone questions you, have a good excuse that's related to your job.

life: with gusto in the beginning and a very obvious loss of steam halfway through. Either way, I found my journal and would love to share snippets of some of the entries with you:

4/11/2010—Eugene, OR

We ended up at a restaurant/bar called Steelhead (I think) and I had some of the best beer ever. Debbie Wunder won a small blender at an auction in the lobby.

4/12/2010—Eugene, Vancouver

It was the first day of the show today and the day we announced the TBS deal. Conan had told me about it last week and I feel like he's really beginning to trust me so I don't want to screw it all up.

4/13/2010—Vancouver

Vancouver is beautiful. All I've seen of it so far has been one street, but it's beautiful. As I write this, I am quite stoned. My nails are red because I got a Canadian manicure, which is exactly the same as a US manicure.

4/15/2010—Vancouver

Conan and I went to a hat store across from the restaurant because they said they would give him a hat for free. He insisted on paying so he ended up buying a weird hat for $120. Then we got in a cab and he told the cab driver that *he was a Greek fisherman and that he likes universal healthcare because it comes in handy when the "nets come back empty."*

4/16/2010—Spokane

After the show Conan wanted to go to this giant red wagon that's in the park next to the venue and there were a mob of people and for the first time on the tour, I got worried. I was a little frazzled, so I decided to go to bed early. Everyone else went to the hotel bar and had a few drinks. They were actually concerned about me the next day since I didn't drink. I love these guys.

4/17/2010—Edmonton

I woke up in Spokane and met Conan and Jeff for breakfast. Then I dragged Conan with me to go on the sky tram ride to see the falls. He created this character, Gertie, who is my ugly sister.

4/19/2010—Seattle

We started our day at the Public Market. Later in the day we went to the Space Needle and went to the very top. We left for the venue and Eddie Vedder destroyed. Backstage he and I kept shooting the shit. At one point I introduced myself and Eddie said, "I know, we've met before at the show." My brain nearly exploded. Everyone left Seattle on such a high.

4/22/2010—San Francisco

We left for San Francisco this morning . . . we got to the hotel and I went out in search of a stuffed parrot. Conan is transforming into a pirate.

4/23/2010—San Francisco

Chris Isaak came back to play with Conan again. I think our guests really love playing in our show.

4/24/2010—Los Angeles

Los Angeles was crazy. We get to the venue and Conan's dressing room has a giant red piano in the middle of it. Then when you walk into the bathroom you first see a duvet to the left and then a giant marble shower with dual shower heads. It was incredible.

It took me a while to realize I had written "duvet" when I meant to write "bidet." It was embarrassing for me to read that.

4/25/2010—Los Angeles

I spent the whole day kicking it with Yaya. Right before call time I went to lunch at Kiwami. Good God I miss good sushi. The show was awesome. The crowd was better than yesterday's. Everyone hung out for drinks after, but again, Conan was swamped with people in his dressing room.

4/29/2010—San Diego

After three days off we went to San Diego. It was a half-hour plane ride. I didn't even know you could take a plane to San Diego. The show had one of the best audiences. We didn't stay and we left for Phoenix that night.

4/30/2010—Phoenix

Conan and I went to the Arizona Biltmore Hotel, which was designed by Frank Lloyd Wright. Ummmm, it was ridiculous (in a good way). I couldn't stop staring at the building. Then on to the show, which was, as usual, GREAT. Las Vegas tonight.

5/1/2010—Las Vegas

We got into Vegas last night and [ex-boyfriend] happened to be in town. Conan talked me out of calling him, which is good. I know he was upset about it and kind of disappointed, but I needed someone to tell me not to see him. Christina, Vero, and Angineh all drove up to stay with me. We went to lunch with Conan and then hung out by the pool. Today's show was a little strange—it was Vegas so there were a lot of douched-out dudes. They were all drunk. After San Diego and Phoenix, our standards were much higher than that. Later on we all went up to Conan's suite, which looked like it belonged to a drug overlord.

5/2/2010—Las Vegas

The girls left and I was at the Craps table gambling away my per diem. Today's audience was so much better. We had Mike Tyson pull the Walker lever and everyone went crazy. After the show everyone was having drinks and I started gambling again. I lost a lot of money.

5/3/2010—Las Vegas

It was our day off and we were in Las Vegas. Conan and I went to a cafe and then I decided to just hang out in my room all day. At night, Gus, Conan, Andy, Sweeney, and I went to a place called Carnevino at the Palazzo. Probably one of the best dinners I've ever had.

5/4/2010—Reno

Reno's theatre was like dinner theatre—there were booths everywhere with tables. It was weird. During the show I went outside to take photos of the video marquee and it wasn't even advertising the show. I stood out there for a while in the cold. When I came back inside I noticed that Sweeney and Matt were at the Craps table and Jeff was at the Black Jack table. No one was watching the show. I didn't have any cash left so I sat with Jeff for a bit.

5/5/2010—San Jose

We all woke up in San Jose and took a van and drove to the Googleplex, which is Google's complex. We get there and there are a ton of eager Google employees who were there to watch a Q&A with Conan. At one point, I went to check out the toilets because they were like ~~duvets~~ bidets attached to the seat. They were actually heated, which blows my mind. You sit directly on the toilets and the goddamn things are heated. Also there's a control panel on the side that distinguishes between "front cleansing," "rear cleansing," and "dryer." So I used it and naturally I started screaming. Andy heard me from outside and talked about it on stage. Everyone at Google laughed at me.

And that's it. My journal ends there. I started off so strong, then just stopped after San Jose. I didn't write about taking a bus to the Winchester Mystery House in San Jose by myself when we had some free time and taking a tour of the property. I was looking at a creepy door that led nowhere when I realized I had to hightail it back to the theater, where it would be call time soon. It wasn't an exciting day, but it would've been nice to write about in my journal.

I didn't write about the band Hanson hanging out in Conan's dressing room in Tulsa before the show and my noticing that they had all . . . grown up. Nicely. Especially the youngest one, Zac, who had been a child when they hit it big and was now quite the dish.

I didn't talk about hanging out backstage in Kansas City, where Jason Sudeikis was a guest, and waiting for his cue with him while he was drinking a Natty Light.

I didn't write about the cool hotel we stayed in while we were in Minneapolis and how Conan had a fun party with the crew in his room.

I completely forgot to write about the shit show that was Atlantic City and how we ate in the casino's staff cafeteria and how I never want to see the underbelly of a casino ever again.

I didn't write about going to New York City and how exciting it was to work on a show at the legendary Radio City Music Hall.

Or how in Boston we went to Conan's twenty-fifth college reunion at Harvard and he participated in a talent show and it was like five hours long. Or how we went to the Lampoon Castle and I invited three members of the Lampoon back to the hotel (nothing scandalous—they just seemed fun) and we ordered hundreds of dollars of room service.

I didn't write about the nightmare that was Bonnaroo. How it was humid and hot as hell and how I saw drunk and high festivalgoers standing under a giant mushroom structure that was spouting water and how, after a day, the water had turned brown and these poor young men and women were getting soaked by this disgusting turd water.

I didn't write about how cool it was to do a show at Third Man Records in Nashville. And how earlier that day we had dropped Conan off at Jack White's house like we were dropping off our child for a playdate.

I never mentioned the tour bus and how my friend Meghan

and I watched *The Human Centipede* on it with the shoddy internet. It took us four hours to watch an hour-and-a-half-long movie, giving me plenty of time to ponder the film's subtle relevance to my industry.

And finally, I didn't talk about our last stop, Atlanta, which happened to be the home of our new network, TBS. We had a meeting with the top brass, and they gave us iPads.

✦

It may seem like I remember a lot of what happened on the tour off the top of my head, but I don't. There are cities and dates that I have completely forgotten. If I hadn't written down that I went to the Space Needle in Seattle, then I wouldn't have remembered that I went. If someone had asked me if I had ever been to the Space Needle and I *hadn't* written it down, I probably would've said no.

So why did I stop keeping the journal, you ask? Why stop documenting all the strange and amazing experiences I was having as Conan's assistant? Because I'm lazy. Because instead of taking five minutes to jot down memories that I can share with my children and grandchildren, I decided to go to the bar every night and try all the fruity drinks the Four Seasons had to offer. I thought, "Hey, this can be my thing. I can be the person who tells others to try the Sugar Rum Fairy at the Austin Four Seasons!" As if hotels keep the same made-up cocktails for years and as if ANYONE CARES. I didn't keep a journal because I was too busy eating free food. I gained twenty-five pounds on that tour, and I really should've seen each pound coming a mile away. When you eat five full meals a day and drink every night, weight is bound to be gained, and boy, was it. Although you know what? Worth. It.

Luckily, Conan's longtime friend Rodman Flender filmed the tour for his documentary *Conan O'Brien Can't Stop*. It feels like someone filmed the best summer camp I've ever been to, and it fills in some of the gaps after my journal left off and where Sugar Rum Fairies erased my memories.

The *Conan O'Brien Can't Stop* Documentary

Have you ever asked yourself, "What does an assistant to an iconic late-night host who had a very well-known exit from a network he was at for sixteen years eat when that late-night host goes on a multicity tour?" Well, I've got the answers for you.

Before I get into it, I just want to say for the record that I am not a television personality. In Conan's orbit, I've found myself in the spotlight more than I ever expected, but still, when a camera is pointed in my boss's direction, I never assume I am in the shot. That explains why I continue to do what I would normally do. When the documentary came out, all I could see was how often I was caught eating on camera. This moving documentary follows a special moment in television history, and according to the video evidence, my part of that history was only to eat. Prominently. The chaos and constant movement of this large tour were all around me, and I spent my time enjoying the free food and drinks, American Express sponsored. In fairness: food is fuel, and an assistant marches on her stomach.

This was filmed during lunch at our first rehearsal. We were still figuring out what the actual show was going to be, and we were supposed to leave in a week. I'm on the left, and half my face is cut off, but I'm taking a massive bite of a piece of medium-rare tri-tip from catering.

I had to sit in so many meetings where the content of the show was discussed. The writers Mike Sweeney and Matt O'Brien would talk to Conan about what the show was going to look like that day. They all worked hard to make the shows as unique to the individual cities as possible. It's the first time I had a good look into Conan's work ethic. No two cities had the same show, and he was involved in every single aspect of what the audience would see. Here I am in one of these key meetings talking into a banana.

As I mentioned, we did shows in Las Vegas, Atlantic City, and Reno. I'm lumping them all together because I lost my per diem in all those cities playing craps. In Las Vegas, I took all $400 of my petty cash and lost it within six minutes. I timed it. It's not that I have a gambling problem. I just love to spend money I pretend isn't mine, even though the petty cash is part of my salary. In the beginning of the tour, I really wanted to make sure I was at every show so I could honestly tell Conan how I felt about it. By the time we went to Reno (the eleventh stop of a thirty-three-city tour), I was wandering around the casino floor looking for a craps table while Conan was onstage. Anyway, here we are in Atlantic City at the Borgata Hotel, where I ordered tuna tartare. I love tuna tartare. This is my first bite.

I look at it lovingly and think, "That's some good tuna tartare."

Here I am with a mouth full of food attempting to stay engaged in the conversation.

Conan is not big on his birthday. I, however, celebrate my "birth month" when October rolls around. It was Conan's birthday on tour, so they got him a cake and gave it to him on the plane. He didn't care about it, but I was clearly looking forward to eating it.

Conan's twenty-fifth college reunion at Harvard coincided with the dates of our tour, so many of us went with him. He walked around the campus where he studied American history and English literature. We visited the dorms where he met his closest friends. We visited the Lampoon Castle and saw the birthplace of Conan's ambitions as a writer and performer. Here I am eating a slice of pizza with a Cambridge police officer.

At Bonnaroo, Conan was obligated to introduce several musicians at the main stage, including Nas and Damian Marley. People had committed him to a variety of appearances and obligations without fully informing him, so he was surprised by the extent of what was expected. This was on top of the two shows he had to perform in a tent at Bonnaroo . . . which was in Tennessee . . . in the middle of June. This all happened at the end of the tour, and Conan had lost so much weight and had overworked himself, both mentally and physically. So many people were excited to see him, and the outpouring of love and support during such a tough time for Conan meant the world not only to him, but to everyone who worked for him. Here I am listening to Mike Sweeney and Conan talk about the intros for the acts at Bonnaroo.

Then my sandwich came. And I remember this sandwich clearly. I remember it was big—way too big. The kind of big where you look at a sandwich and try to figure out a strategy. Do you bite toast to toast in one big bite? Or do you do two small bites? Here's the strategy I went for.

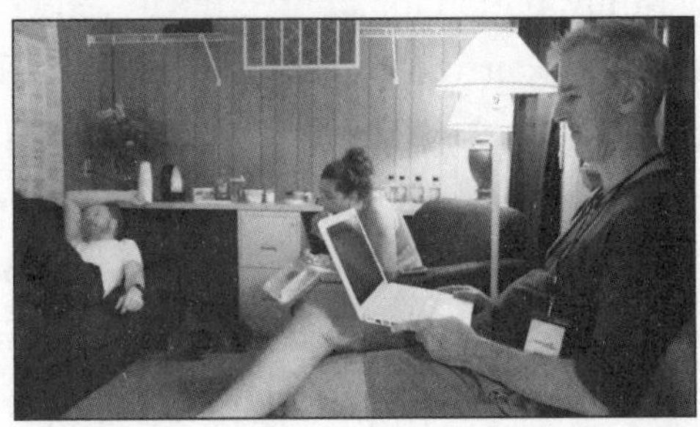

And that was my experience on the tour. I'm grateful that these moments were captured on film so my family can see what I was able to accomplish during a pivotal moment in my boss's career.

Was I emotionally there for Conan as he was struggling with the realization that his time at the network that helped him build his late-night legacy had come to an end? Most of the time yes, and I had a mouth full of food while I was doing it.

The White House Correspondents' Dinner

In 2013, Conan was tapped to host the White House Correspondents' Dinner. Of all the great events I got to attend, the White House Correspondents' Dinner was the most exciting one for me. It was where everyone from politics, media, and the entertainment industry would converge and interact with one another. It was a massive ball in a massive ballroom, and I was thrilled to have an opportunity to go.

Though my work ethic can often lack, Conan's and Mike Sweeney's work ethics are astounding. They are both already so naturally funny, but on top of their innate senses of humor, they care deeply about the comedy they create. This is why they worked on Conan's White House Correspondents' Dinner speech up until the absolute last minute. This type of work ethic, however, poses a problem for at least one person: the person who is walking aimlessly around the hotel waiting for the final notes. The same person who ends up spending ages looking for the business center so she can print out the speech on a series of notecards from which Conan is going to read. Who was that chump, you ask? Why, it was me.

We were all getting ready in the hotel where the dinner was taking place, so it was chaos. The first time I went down to the business center to print the notes, it was just the staff preparing the room for the guests and I felt no sense of urgency. I remember printing out the cards, then checking to make sure they were all in the proper order and casually reading some and chuckling. Here are some of my favorite jokes from Conan's speech:

> *But President Obama, you had some great jokes and it was a pleasure watching you stand up here and do what I do. So now it's only fair that I get to do what you do. That's right, ladies and gentlemen, for the next fifteen minutes, I'll be mired in a tense, dysfunctional standoff with Congress.*

> *Congratulations to C-SPAN for winning the bid to broadcast this event. They narrowly beat out HGTV 2, QVC South America, and the Hilton Hotel "How to Check Out" channel.*

> *But as I look out at all of the media here with us tonight, I realize this is all just one big high school cafeteria. Think about it: Fox is the jocks, MSNBC is the nerds, bloggers are the goths, NPR is the table for kids with peanut allergies, Al Jazeera is the weird foreign exchange student that nobody*

talks to. And print media, I didn't forget you, you're that poor kid who died sophomore year in a car crash. (But cheer up: we dedicated the yearbook to you.)

It's hard to believe the Republicans didn't fare better in the election with the support of celebrities like Ted Nugent and Meatloaf. I guess they overestimated the number of voters who still drive carpeted vans.

There's RNC chairman Reince Priebus. You heard me correctly, his name is Reince Priebus. Tonight he's sitting right in between his brothers "Lather Priebus" and "Repeat Priebus."

It's no surprise that Speaker John Boehner isn't here tonight. Speaker Boehner and President Obama are still struggling to get along. President Obama and John Boehner are like a blind date between Anderson Cooper and Rachel Maddow. In theory, they understand each other's positions, but deep down you know that's never going to happen.

I would print the speech, go back to the room, Sweeney and Conan would make changes, and I would head back downstairs to the business center to print the speech again. This happened so many times, and over the course of so many hours, I began, uncharacteristically, to feel the sense of urgency I'd initially lacked. I didn't have time to check anything. I would print, grab the cards, and just glance through them in the elevator on the way up, praying they were all okay. The Secret

Service eventually came into the picture. Because the president of the United States was going to be there, keeping disheveled-looking young women who were walking around in flip-flops and holding a mountain of blue notecards away from the main ballroom was literally their job. Unfortunately, the ballroom happened to be steps away from the business center.

When I walked down to print out the speech for the umpteenth time, a nice but stern Secret Service agent stopped me and began asking a series of questions.

"Are you a guest in the hotel?"

"No, but we have a couple rooms here because I work for Conan O'Brien and he's speaking tonight."

He looks me up and down suspiciously. "Do you have any identification?"

"I don't, but I promise I work for him. This is his speech tonight," I say as I hold up a pile of blue notecards with jokes on them.

After a few more questions, he lets me access the business center, but not before he says, "The next time you come down here, you need to be wearing a dress or whatever outfit you're wearing tonight."

"Of course. Thank you so much, sir. I promise I won't let you down." Followed by a giggle and a smile because flirting never hurt anyone.

I walk toward the business center and realize it's now cocktail hour for the dinner, because everyone—meaning all of Hollywood's and Washington's power players—is meandering around near the business center, and I'm sticking out big-time.

People are wearing stunning gowns and tuxedos, and I'm in my jeans, T-shirt, and flip-flops looking like a complete dick. When I get to the business center, after printing out this speech countless times, the printer is suddenly not working. It's stressful enough to print out a speech that some of the most important people in politics and news will listen to, but it's another thing when you need to figure out the settings to get everything printed on five-by-seven blue notecards.

I'm sweating.

Sweeney is calling me to ask me why I'm taking so long. It's nearly time for Conan and a few others to head to a predinner meet and greet with President Obama, and I'm holding everyone up.

I sweat even more.

At this point, there are several hotel staffers trying to help me with the printer. It keeps jamming, and I keep mentally updating my résumé.

After what feels like an eternity, we get it to work and I run back upstairs and again there are changes. This is the last time, I'm told.

I remember what the Secret Service agent told me, so I put on my dress, but there's no way I'm running around in heels, so I stick on my flip-flops again. When I get back downstairs, I nod at the Secret Service agent and gesture to my dress. He does not remember me, but he lets me through.

I print out the speech one final time. At this point, the hotel staff working in the business center have become my best friends. We've bonded so much through my trauma that

I think about suggesting we all get matching tattoos that say "I survived the WHCD 2013" alongside a graphic of a printer.

When I finally leave the business center for the last time, I give a thumbs-up to the hotel staffer sitting at the table and say, "This will probably be the last time I come down here tonight!"

He barely looks up from his computer and says, uneventfully, "Have a lovely evening."

I stand there awkwardly, hoping he'll give me more. He doesn't. I'm glad then that we didn't get the tattoos.

I go back upstairs and hand Conan all the cards. He and Sweeney express their gratitude, and then everyone leaves and I'm there. Alone.

This is what my job is—a night where I stress out over the smallest of mishaps because I understand the stakes. The mishaps are guaranteed. The consequences could actually be as severe as ruining Conan's White House Correspondents' Dinner speech. But no one sees that part. They just see me leave the hotel room, then come back with all the blue notecards they need. If they notice the sweat or the flip-flops, no one ever says.

Conan delivered his speech and did a great job, and I wanted to get up there during the applause and say, "I printed that speech!" Even as I type this recollection, I realize how uneventful it must seem. Well, to everyone except the assistants in the room, who I'm sure can feel my stress viscerally. But those hiccups are all I remember. I don't remember who I saw or what conversations I had. I don't even remember what I ate, and food is so important to me.

The dinner reminds me of a time when I was still working at NBC. We were doing a press event at the Langham in Pasadena, and I was told John Stamos needed access to one of the hotel rooms in order to rest before his interview. My boss told me they didn't have any empty rooms left and that I would have to give his publicist my key. My room hadn't been serviced yet that day, so I ran up to make it Stamos-ready. My friend was in there using the space to get ready for the press event, and I stormed into the room and yelled, "We need to get all this shit out of here! Stamos is coming!"

It was pure panic. We then cleaned the room at a terrifyingly quick pace, realizing the only thing standing between John Stamos and a nap was the two of us. We scrubbed and tidied and hoped he wouldn't be able to tell the bed had been slept in. As soon as we were done, I ran down to the bar where I had been told Stamos's publicist was waiting, and I went in, walked up to the bar where she was having a drink, and proudly presented the key for the room and said, "This is for you."

"What is this for?" she responded.

"I was told John Stamos needed a room to rest in before the interview, so this is the key for the room."

"Oh, thanks. He doesn't need it anymore," she said as she took a sip of her drink.

John Fucking Stamos.

Again, no one understood the stress and panic that went on behind the scenes. They asked for the key and they got the key and that was all they knew.

Over time, the stress and panic I would feel in these situations dissipated. They stopped as soon as I realized what I needed to get done would get done even if I stayed relaxed.

Soon after this change, I would be *too* relaxed, and Conan would get upset because he took it as a sign that I didn't care enough—that being at ease meant I didn't feel the urgency that was necessary in certain situations. And he was right. I overcompensated. It takes A LOT for me to get nervous now. John Stamos needs a room? Cool, he'll get one when it's ready. Conan O'Brien needs his White House Correspondents' Dinner speech printed out? Neat, I'll put on my dress and grab my ticket so I can easily get past the Secret Service and I'll take care of that as soon as I can.

This is the dawn of a new day, one in which I'll sit down next to Stamos's publicist and grab a few drinks. Then, when I'm ready, I'll do what needs to be done. If you're thinking, "Gee, Sona, this sounds like an awful approach to work," you're right. I'll never get hired for another job . . . but at least I won't be stressed about it.

Filler

I was hiking with my friend Liesel when she told me to write this book. I thought, "Great! Maybe I can make enough money to remodel my kitchen." What I didn't think about was how much *work* this was going to be. I don't know why I thought writing a book would be easy, but it's not. Plus, I have a set number of words I have to write, and I procrastinated so much that I am now scrambling to get it all done. Since I wrote my proposal, a global pandemic hit, and I bought a house, got knocked up, and had two adorable, fat babies. This is a filler section. It's complete nonsense. I'm just typing out words so I can add them to my word count. I'm so bad at completing the tasks I have to complete that in this professional venture, I'm dedicating an entire section to filler.

Procrastinating has always been an issue for me. As a refresher for many of you, "procrastination" is defined as "the action of delaying or postponing something." What was I doing instead of writing this book, you may ask? I went through a foreign language phase on Netflix. I started with the Spanish series *Money Heist*, then watched the French show *Call My Agent!* and finished it up with the Italian series *Summertime*. Whenever I finished these shows, I would feel like I was fluent in the languages. "Fluent" is defined as "being able to express oneself easily and articulately."

I also watched all seasons of *The Great British Baking Show* and *Derry Girls*. Although they are in English, I felt the sudden urge to speak in an accent.

Watching these shows reminded me of the time I was in Japan for my honeymoon. My husband and I went out drinking in the Golden Gai district of Tokyo and stumbled into this bar. We drank all night with a Catalonian, a Brit, two Australians, and one other American. The bartender had a toy alligator, and you would press down on its teeth one by one, and the person who pressed on the tooth that forced the mouth to close would lose, only we started gambling and whoever pressed the tooth that forced the mouth to close would win the pot. I lost $200.

We were in Japan at the same time Conan was there for a Conan Without Borders special. I stopped traveling with Conan to film the specials after Mexico. It became clear early on that I wasn't really necessary. I also could never resign myself to the idea that I couldn't fully explore the countries like I wanted to—we would go to locations and shoot there for hours. It wasn't a vacation; it was work. Really fun work, but work nonetheless. When we were filming in Cuba, I disappeared for an hour and bought a painting. It took forever for me to find the rest of the crew, and I realized I couldn't just aimlessly walk around in a foreign country without having a concrete plan as to how I'd get back to my colleagues. Anyway, after talking to Conan and Jeff Ross, we decided it would probably be better if I stopped traveling with everyone to film the Conan Without Borders series. I didn't contribute anything to the traveling crew. No one noticed my absence.

When I was in college, I procrastinated all the time (like so many of you who are reading this, because if you bought a book called *The World's Worst Assistant*, then chances are you can relate). I once pulled an all-nighter and wrote a twelve-page, heavily sourced paper for my Ideology and Propaganda class at USC. I got an A. I don't change my behavior because I don't suffer the consequences, and it's so hard to get motivated when I can take a couple edibles and watch *Step Brothers* for the thirtieth time instead of doing the work I'm supposed to do. *Step Brothers* is a 2008 film starring Will Ferrell and John C. Reilly. It's about two unmotivated, unemployed grown men who still live at home and become stepbrothers once their parents get married. They're delightful morons, and I guess to a certain extent I see myself in them. I, too, would rub my testicles all over someone's drum kit in an effort to antagonize them (if I had testicles, of course . . . I don't).

Anyway, I took up knitting during the pandemic. I got so wrapped up in it that I started to binge *Grace and Frankie* so I could have something fun on while I knit. Knitting became a huge distraction for me, and I told my friend Erica that I would knit a scarf for her and I was on my way until I ran out of yarn. I had made the scarf way too wide, so now I have a short, wide scarf—like a chode. I put it in a drawer and never got back to it, so that's another project I never finished. *Grace and Frankie* is a show on Netflix following two women in their golden years who discovered their husbands have been cheating on them with each other. It stars Jane Fonda, Lily Tomlin, Martin Sheen, and Sam Waterston. My neighbor works on it.

Let's see . . . what else? I have a lot of perks in my job. I get to keep all the gifts Conan doesn't want, and people send him some really nice things. Whenever Conan and I have to run an errand together, I look for the most expensive restaurant nearby where we can eat afterward. I've stayed in some really nice hotels, and it has broken me. My real life and my work life are so different in terms of travel accommodations. I remember staying at a Four Seasons for work and the following week going on a personal trip and staying in a yurt in someone's backyard that I found on Airbnb. When we first checked in, my husband and I heard people having sex in the main house. We looked up toward the bedroom window and saw two naked people looking down at us. Other than that, the yurt was cute, but it wasn't the Four Seasons.

I wonder if I can change the formatting in a book. If I write with a bigger font and wider margins, I wonder if that will translate into the actual publication of this book. I don't know how to increase margins on a single page of a book, so here we are.

Going back to my life as an assistant vs. my normal life, I remember I had never flown in a class higher than coach before, and when we went on the tour, I started flying private to all our tour locations. The last stop of the tour was Atlanta, and the plane American Express sponsored for us would be taking Conan back to his family and the rest of us would have to fly commercial back to LA. As a gift, they flew me back first class. When I stepped into the first-class cabin, I was appalled at how close the seats were to each other. After two short months of flying private, it became all I would tolerate. I was insufferable. The reality of my life is coach, however. I have coach money. I'm not Beyoncé. I don't have the financial capability to fly private, so the adjustment back to what I'm used to was inevitable. It's like taking a hen that's been in a coop her whole life, letting her fly private for two months, then putting her back in the coop. Part of the reason this filler section exists is so I can get closer to the word count I agreed to in my contract. Then maybe I'll make private jet money. Just kidding. I won't.

This is all I can do. Surprisingly, this has been one of my favorite parts to write. I've heard Stephen King's process is to just start writing a novel and see where it takes him. This section is clearly inspired by that philosophy. I guess I'm like Stephen King. I'm sure he has private jet money.

PART TWO

After finishing her third episode of The Office *for the morning, Sona decides to go to the kitchen and fix herself a snack. As she walks to the kitchen, she can't help but feel like she's forgetting to do something. What was it that Conan had asked of her? She'll remember eventually, but she hasn't yet.*

She walks into the kitchen, and the interns are all talking about a new app she's never heard of. The kitchen is where all the interns sit, and there's always a hint of embarrassment when walking in because she knows she's getting more and more out of touch. She doesn't know what happened, but one day she woke up and didn't understand what they were talking about or how to join in. She has to go into the kitchen for the bagels, though. And sometimes there are peanut M&M's. Every once in a while, they'll have Cheez-Its. And on a good week, there's a lot of white cheddar popcorn. It's worth the risk.

She walks in.

> **SONA:** (trying to slip into the conversation seamlessly, but coming off painfully old) Kanye, huh? He's crazy.

> **AN INTERN:** Uh, yeah.

That's it. That's all she has, and now she's awkwardly standing there as six of them watch her cut a bagel, then stick it in the toaster. Good God, she has to wait for it to toast now. It's all so awful.

> **AN INTERN:** How's your day so far?

> **SONA:** It's good! Conan came in and asked me to do something and it sounded important and I completely forgot what it was.

The interns are there to learn and they are learning nothing.

Sona looks back at the toaster. Is this the only toaster in the world that takes this long? She can't believe how long this is taking. It's complete agony. There's total silence in the kitchen as six young, eager college students watch Sona watch her toast toasting in the toaster. Finally one chirps up—

AN INTERN: Are you worried he'll be mad?

SONA: Not really. I'm sure I'll remember what he wants eventually.

The toaster dings. There is no sound in the world more glorious. She gets the cream cheese from the fridge. The interns watch as she glops the cream cheese on her bagel. Is it too much? Is the bagel too hot, and is the cream cheese melting? Does she look like an asshole?

SONA: Did you guys know Michael B. Jordan is filming something here?

AN INTERN: Yes!

SONA: He was driving on the lot the other day and stopped a friend of mine while she was walking so he could tell her she was beautiful. Then he drove off.

The interns collectively gasp. Sona did it. She impressed the interns. Just in time, too—her bagel is fully cream-cheesed and she's ready to leave the kitchen. And now she wants to visit her friend Erica. She visits her every day.

SONA: Bye, guys!

Sona leaves the kitchen and veers toward Erica's desk.

SONA: Hi, Erica!

Erica keeps her head down. She knows if she acts busy this will deter Sona from staying at her desk too long.

ERICA: Hey!

Erica then looks back at her computer, visibly busy. Sona leans further down over her cubicle wall.

SONA: Are you working?

ERICA: Yes.

SONA: Do you need a hug?

ERICA: Ugh, fine. But you know the rules. No longer than three seconds.

Sona hugs Erica as she sits there limp. Sona always hugs too hard and closes her eyes. Erica is a professional. While

Sona is the quintessential extrovert, Erica is an introvert. They are opposites as people, but by visiting Erica's desk every day when they first started working together, Sona broke Erica down, and now Erica will never be able to get rid of her.

ERICA: One . . . two . . . three . . . Okay, that's enough.

Sona lets go. She appreciates these small victories.

SONA: Okay, I'm going to go back to my desk now. Maybe Queen Elizabeth and Prince Philip will give you a call later.

ERICA: Please no.

Sona goes back to her desk with her bagel. She sits down and promptly calls Erica. Erica sees her calling and picks up reluctantly.

ERICA: What?

SONA: (in an awful English accent that sounds like the part of *Mrs. Doubtfire* where she has a plate of whipped cream on her face and shoots up behind the refrigerator and yells "He-llo!") Erica, this is Queen Elizabeth. I'm calling from London, England.

ERICA: This is awful.

SONA: (her voice is getting higher, the English accent is getting more offensive) I just wanted to tell you that if you were ever in London, you should come to Buckingham Palace for some tea and crumpets. It'll be most splendid!

ERICA: Can I just hang up, please?

SONA: (her impression at its absolute worst) Hold on, Prince Philip wants to talk to you. (Sona switches to another awful English accent that sounds like a combination of Darrell Hammond doing a Sean Connery impression on *SNL*, John Lithgow's Winston Churchill from *The Crown*, and a little bit of Neil Diamond singing "America.") Erica! This is Prince Philip. I was just out hunting pheasants.

ERICA: Wow. Okay.

SONA: (as Prince Philip in a way Prince Philip has never sounded) Anyway, as the queen, my wife, said, you should come over one day and hang out.

ERICA: "Hang out"? This is a waste of both our time.

SONA: (incoherently, terribly, and offensively British) It was lovely talking to you, Erica. Uh, goodbye!

Sona hangs up the phone and chuckles to herself. She looks at her email, and she has sixty-eight unread messages. It's time to do some work, or Conan is going to know she doesn't remember what he asked her to do. She repeats her mantra: "It'll come to me eventually."

PROFESSIONALISM

I'VE INTERACTED WITH PEOPLE FROM NEWS, POLITICS, ENTERtainment, and so many other fields. Professionalism is key if you want to be taken seriously. On email or on the phone with strangers, my tone changes. I'm a different person. Sometimes I think it would be hilarious if Conan were the only person privy to how unprofessional I can be—as if he's yelling into an abyss about how unprofessional I am and everyone else is thinking, "That's not my experience with her. In fact, I found her to be quite impressive."

So what is professionalism? I've learned it's being cognizant of the people you're interacting with and keeping a very specific line between who you really are and who you should be in a work environment. Someone who was doing keg stands on Saturday will roll into work on Monday and write an email that includes the phrases "we'll circle back" and "we can cross that bridge when we get to it." I am one of those people. At work, I find myself laughing too hard at the slightest hint of humor. I've said the phrase "get down to brass tacks" to more people than I'd like to admit.

But with Conan and me, as his assistant, our professionalism eroded not long after I started. Instead of allowing Conan to make jokes at my expense without reacting, I started to engage. That was my first mistake. Then, before I knew it, I was calling him a dick on camera, and he was calling me a crazy Armenian.

And my lack of professionalism wasn't just directed at Conan. One day, my friend at work Dixon was eating some popcorn. I saw him holding a bunch in his hand, and I walked up to him and smacked all the popcorn out of his hand and started laughing at him. I did to him what Conan does to me every day. I continued the cycle of psychopathy. Anyway, later that day, Dixon saw me walking in the parking structure and thought it was the best time for him to get me back for my joke. He yelled out his window, "I'll get you, you stupid bitch!" Only it wasn't me. The woman looked like me from behind, but it wasn't until he had yelled what he had yelled that he drove past her and saw that it wasn't me. Sometimes I think about how terrified that woman must've been, just walking along and minding her own business, then having someone in a Mini Cooper scream obscenities at her in the parking structure. I hope she's okay.

Anyway, I grew up with a strong work ethic. My parents instilled the importance of work into both my brother and me—all based in an urgent need to get ahead that is found so often in immigrant communities. We both started working at a young age, and we were punctual and respectful—other than the time I got fired from the Hollywood Bowl, of course. The older I got, the less I gave in to professional conformity. That's when I started to take notice of how the job was servicing *me* and not vice versa. Sure, this job pays well, but do I *want* to come in on Mondays? My mental well-being took precedence, and my freedom to be myself was the new priority. And I am not a professional person at work. I like to do my work but also have fun. I know that means there are some careers I'm not cut out for—DMV worker, Supreme Court justice, commercial pilot, neurosurgeon, nanny—but in most jobs I've found it's entirely possible to find the right balance.

Now my parents look at what's become of me—their daughter is literally writing a book about her experience as a TV assistant called *The World's Worst Assistant*. They're horrified I call Conan all kinds of names in public, but that's the environment that was created and it's the environment I've embraced. This is the new American dream.

Stalking

Every once in a while, someone comes on the show who I'm genuinely excited about. Not that every guest isn't a thrill, but some are more exciting to me than others. By chance, they're usually always men and they're usually always attractive.

I tend to do the same thing every time: I dress up extra cute that day and spend extra time doing my hair and makeup, as if they'll see me and care, and I always end up in the green room before the show, even though most of the time I watch the show from my desk. And yet, even with all that effort, I hide as soon as they walk in, as if I'm playing coy. I don't want to seem too eager, otherwise they won't fall in love with me, so instead I play hard to get. Has it ever worked, you ask? Fuck no. Why would that idiotic approach work? I'll paint you a picture:

So I've always loved Slash. He was one of my first crushes ever since he walked out of that chapel in those leather pants and jacket with no shirt on in the "November Rain" video and tore it up on that guitar. He's part of the reason I married someone who can play the guitar. He would come by the show often because he knew Jimmy Vivino pretty well, and he would do bits on the show every once in a while. When he walked into the green room, I would immediately place myself behind a large plant. I wanted a place that was covert enough for him to kind of see me but transparent enough for *me* to clearly see *him*. I would stand there drooling and breathing heavily until he was called onto the stage for whatever he was doing. Then I would emerge from behind the plant and act like nothing was out of the ordinary. I would watch all attractive guys I have a crush on from behind a plant in the green room.

Quick sidenote: Conan once hosted the Warner Bros. panel at Comic-Con. It was the year both *Justice League* and *King Arthur: Legend of the Sword* were coming out. I went with Conan to the San Diego Convention Center, and I was in a holding area while Conan was in Hall H commencing his hosting duties. At one point, I had to get something we'd left behind in the car, so I took the elevator down and grabbed it. On the way back up, I was in the elevator, and as the doors were closing, a big, beautiful hand reached in and stopped them. In walked Henry Cavill followed by Charlie Hunnam. It was just the three of us in the elevator and I was sweating. It was a quick ride, but it felt an hour long. They were talking to each other, and if you held a gun to my head now, I couldn't tell you a single word that passed between them because I was so mesmerized by their handsome faces. It was like the time my junior high crush asked me if he could borrow a pencil and all I remember was looking down at his hands and muttering a pathetic "sure." I then remember telling him to follow me to the classroom where I had already put all my stuff and then reaching into my pencil box, which was emblazoned with Pekkle, a Sanrio character, and giving him my favorite pencil, which I thought he'd appreciate. Although, thinking about it now, how the fuck would he know that was my favorite pencil? It was my chance and I blew it by being a complete loser, and I felt like I was doing that again in the elevator. An icebreaker like a confident "Love your work" to both of them could've been a game changer. But no, instead I stood there sweating and staring. And then they left. I had never wanted a plant to be in an elevator so badly.

Anyway, the reason I bring up my green room technique is because it came in handy when Conan hosted the CORE Gala in the beginning of 2020 and Leonardo DiCaprio was among the attendees. I hadn't realized Leonardo DiCaprio would be there until I was searching for a restroom and walked down to a lower level and saw him look up to see if I was someone important (naturally, he went back to his conversation as soon as he realized I was not). Because Conan was hosting the event, I was expected to be on hand backstage in case he needed me to get Mike Sweeney or a drink or a snack or whatever else. Instead I spent the majority of the night stalking Leonardo DiCaprio.

When Leo took a break to catch up with a friend outside, who was there behind a plant? Yup, yours truly.

When he was at the bar getting a refreshing beverage, who was nearby also getting a drink? That's right, me again.

When he was chatting with Julia Roberts, who was sitting at a nearby table where she wasn't assigned, just covertly staring? You guessed it! Me.

That was my whole night. It was like a dance only one of us knew we were having. I had zero intention of speaking to him or interacting with him in any way. I just wanted to look at him. Now that I type it out, I realize how creepy it is. I shouldn't be working in the entertainment industry. Especially not in a job where I am constantly meeting, helping, and otherwise interacting with major celebrities. But really, I'm more a danger to myself than to anyone else.

After a substantial amount of stalking, I realized I had done enough. There was a point where I had to reflect on what I'd done all night. I had ignored my work responsibilities because I was too busy following around a movie star just to *look* at him. And I wasn't a teenager who was following around the Beatles—I was a grown adult woman who had a mortgage. I was at a work event.

So instead of continuing to follow him, midway through the night I changed my approach. I sat at my table, positioned myself so the centerpiece would be blocking me, and just stared at him from my seat like a normal person. I can't remember how Conan did that night, but I'm sure I told him he did a great job.

Golf Carts

Employees at both the Universal and Warner Bros. lots use golf carts to easily get around their massive campuses. They're zippy and fun and an easy way to get from point A to point B on a big movie lot. They're also so quintessentially a Hollywood tool—you see executives and stars getting around in golf carts in movies made about movies. It was exciting when I first knew I'd have one at my disposal, but I quickly learned golf carts are no joke.

Here are three different stories involving golf carts. One doesn't involve me at all, but like the others, it's a great example of professionalism. Or lack thereof.

A Golf Cart Love Story

In 2009, when Conan was filming *The Tonight Show* at the Universal lot, two of our interns took a golf cart out on an errand and one came back injured. The intern driving (we'll call him Jack) had a crush on the passenger intern (we'll call her

Rose . . . yes, after the movie, because any prospect of romance sank like the *Titanic* after this golf cart ride). To get back to the office as quickly as possible—and in an effort to impress Rose—Jack took full advantage of the hilly terrain of the Universal lot and pretended he was driving a Chevy Corvette on an open road. Although golf carts can only go so fast, when you're heading down on an incline, speed builds. When there are no doors or windows, speed building is not always a good thing. Rose was having a blast at first, enjoying the backlot at Universal zipping by at a whopping 20 mph. It quickly became pretty clear, however, that Jack was losing control the steeper the hills got. The look of joy on their faces turned to dread as they realized their vulnerability. Even worse—a turn was coming up. Jack braced himself as he took the left turn far too fast . . . barely keeping the golf cart from flipping over. Once the turn was done, he breathed a sigh of relief and looked over to Rose to gauge her reaction, only she wasn't there.

She had flown out of the golf cart.

Not a graceful tuck and roll or a harmless tumble—she was thrown out of the golf cart like a rag doll. Like she was made of straw. She was clearly injured, and Jack looked at her body on the ground knowing any prospect of him asking her out had vanished as she lay there bleeding and moaning from pain.

What's worse is someone on a nearby tour tram had seen and stopped the tram to see if she was okay. The entire tram of tourists sat there with their mouths agape and cameras clicking. What a joy it must've been for them to travel all the way to Los Angeles from wherever they were and get a tour on a real live movie lot, then witness a college student take a turn too fast and a second college student fly out of the moving golf cart with the words "THE TONIGHT SHOW WITH CONAN O'BRIEN" emblazoned on the side in massive letters. They probably thought it was a part of some stunt show.

The tram tour guide called the lot's security, and multiple security golf carts and the lot's firefighters all showed up, also in golf carts. They tended to Rose's injuries and asked Jack a ton of questions about what happened. Because the golf cart belonged to the show, our office coordinator got a call, and before long everyone at the show had heard what happened. Once we knew Rose was okay, the tables turned on Jack. No one had ever heard of someone blowing their chance with a crush because they were responsible for them flying out of a moving golf cart before. We made fun of him relentlessly for the rest of his internship.

When Conan's Children Were Stuck in a Lagoon

Interns aren't the only ones who abuse the golf carts. I, too, have had mishaps with them. And I'm not talking about the time a few of us took the golf cart out of the lot and drove it on the street to get ramen. We took them at their word when they called our golf carts "street legal," and before we knew it, there were angry drivers tailing us in their Chevy Tahoes because we were holding up traffic on Barham Boulevard. We were just begging to get killed on the road, but we went and had ramen and returned without any injuries.

But I'm not talking about one of those times. I'm talking about the time I was giving Conan's children a tour of the lot on the golf cart and got stuck in a hole.

When Conan's children, Neve and Beckett, came to visit him at work, it was the only time I was ever truly on my A game. They would get dropped off, spend the day sitting in on meetings and hanging out with their dad, and if he had to go do something they couldn't join in on, I would play video games with them or take them around the lot. On this particular day, I decided it would be a good idea to give them a tour of the Warner Bros. backlot.

The backlot is fun to explore—you can see houses from *Full House* and *Gilmore Girls*, drive around where they did exterior shots for *Friends* and *ER*, and see the famous Warner Bros. water tower. There's also a lagoon.

According to my friend who was a tour guide on the Warner Bros. lot, the lagoon was used for *Jurassic Park*, *ER*, *Gilmore Girls*, *Pretty Little Liars*, and so many other productions. It's near where they would shoot exterior shots for *True Blood*. On the day I gave Conan's kids a tour, however, the lagoon was empty. It was a large empty hole surrounded by trees. So for reasons I still don't understand, I thought it would be a good idea to drive into the hole. Maybe to get a better look? Maybe because it was empty and seemed inviting? Or maybe it's because I'm just very dumb.

So when I took Neve and Beckett, who at the time were ten and eight years old respectively, into the empty, sunken-in expanse, I thought they would think it was cool. And it was. When we tried to get out, however, the golf cart couldn't handle the incline out of the hole. We would back up, build up momentum, drive halfway up the hill to get back to the main road, then slowly slide back down into the empty lagoon. We did this far more times than I'd like to admit. At one point, I asked Neve and Beckett to get out of the golf cart to lower the amount of weight in it, thinking that would help. But if I had to bet on who out of the three of us was weighing down the golf cart, it wouldn't be the two children. It would be the grown woman who got them in the hole in the first place.

No one drove by, so we were on our own. Luckily, instead of thinking I was pathetic, they thought it was funny. At first, I did, too, but then I started to worry about how I would ever get this stupid golf cart out of this empty lagoon. I considered leaving it there and sending interns to pick it up and letting them figure it out, but it was a bit of a walk back to the lot, and like all of Conan's show's golf carts, this one had "CONAN" stuck to it in massive letters. There would have been too many questions. I even thought about teaching Neve how to drive a golf cart so she could drive it up herself—maybe the lack of my weight would allow the cart to go faster. It didn't take long to understand why that was a terrible idea. After a while, I realized what needed to be done: I needed to ask Conan's kids to help me push the golf cart out of the empty lagoon.

So these precious children stood behind the golf cart with

me and pushed with all of their elementary school might. They barely helped. I basically did everything, but it was nice to let them feel like they were making a difference. After a surprisingly long time of being stuck in this giant empty lagoon, we finally were able to get the golf cart back out onto the main road.

This might be the first time Conan is ever hearing about this story in full. I think at the time when Neve and Beckett were recounting to him the harrowing adventure we'd had, I played it down and made it seem like we were barely stuck and we were out in minutes.

Conan, if you're reading this, your children were never in any real danger. Imagine driving a vehicle into a giant empty pool, then being stuck in the pool and not knowing how to get out of it because the vehicle can't handle the incline back up. That's what this was.

After that golf cart ride, Neve, Beckett, and I would stick to endless races in *Mario Kart* instead of any adventures outside. It was safer that way.

A Golf Cart and a Police Car

On more than one occasion, I would go out with work friends after we were done for the day, drink too much, then find a way to get home without driving. My early days with Conan were before Uber and Lyft existed, so I always had to ask someone who lived near me to give me a ride home.

My friend Lindsay Sheehan was executive producer Jeff Ross's assistant for a few years, and she and I went out for a sushi dinner after work one day, had too many drinks, slept on Jeff's sectional in his office, and drove home in the morning.

Another time, I had a bit too much to drink at the Smoke House down the street from the Warner Bros. lot and threw up in the parking structure at work.

There was also the time when I met up with an old friend from NBC and had too much to drink and left my car at the bar, then asked the interns to pick it up for me the next day. I mentioned this on a remote Conan did when he was meeting with the interns.

This one time, however, my friends and I went out to dinner and they all had a couple drinks—I was the designated driver, so I was sober. When we walked back to the Universal lot, we noticed there was a police car sitting in front of our studio.

That day we had done a bit on the show with the police car, and our props department left it out front so they could return it the next day. They also left the keys in the car. So we got into the car and drove it around our studio. We felt no shame.

As we were making a turn, however, we saw a security guard who was working the night shift. Even though we were going about 5 mph in the car, we got incredibly nervous and just stopped in the middle of the road. Just a dead stop.

So if you're this security guard, imagine walking around a dead lot in the middle of the night. You never see any action because you're stuck with the graveyard shift. Then suddenly you look up and see a random police car driving at a staggeringly slow speed around the *Tonight Show* soundstage, which makes no sense since the lot uses their own security team. Then the police car just stops for no reason in the middle of the road.

We had to think of something so the security guard wouldn't approach the vehicle. We knew if he saw us driving around, we could be in trouble because we were driving a police car and we weren't the police. I couldn't think of anything else to do, so I just stuck my hand out of the car and waved at him. A familiar, confident wave that I was hoping conveyed the message "Hey there, fellow security official."

It didn't matter that there were three young ladies in the car who were dressed in civilian clothing. It didn't matter that a police car had no place on the Universal lot in the middle of the night. All that mattered to this security guard was that if anything was suspect, then I wouldn't have waved at him so confidently. After a brief pause, the security guard reluctantly raised his hand and waved back at us. I thank a misspent youth for this stroke of genius.

I then pressed on the gas and turned back toward the studio, creeping away at 5 mph. The security guard looking at us, knowing something was fishy but realizing his salary didn't give him enough impetus to care.

When we got back to the studio, we did a photo shoot with the police car, sent the photos to our props department, then looked over and saw the golf cart sitting there.

The really fun thing about working on the Universal lot is that the backlot is very well-known. It's a theme park ride. People come from all over the world to see the Universal lot and take the backlot tram tour. We were lucky enough to have access to it every time we went into work. After we parked the police car, we realized that had just been our first ride. It was time for us to tour the backlot in the golf cart.

We drove to the house where Norman Bates lived and considered going inside (in the end we got too scared). We then moseyed on over to the Bates Motel and considered pretending we were checking in (we got too scared again). We eventually made it to Courthouse Square, where *Back to the Future* and many other films and TV shows were shot. We defiled the famed Universal backlot tour. We didn't care. We couldn't see the security guard anywhere.

✦

Although mobility on the lot might not seem like a big deal, for me, the freedom of comfortably getting around made the lots I've worked on my personal playgrounds. While some people may respect the set of an Alfred Hitchcock masterpiece as hallowed ground, I liked to think it was put there for me to enjoy, to frolic around with my friends. Almost like Hitchcock made *Psycho* just so that, fifty years later, my idiot friends and I could drive around on a golf cart taking photos with the set. Some people look at having access to these locations that housed legendary productions as a test of their personal responsibility to preserve the sanctity of said locations. I, on the other hand, find the thrill is using them for my own photo shoots. Because I'm a professional.

Business Trips

In October 2010, a month before we were set to premiere Conan's new show on TBS, American Express approached Conan about shooting a couple commercials for their brand. After collaborating with their ad team, one of the ideas Conan's writers proposed had him flying to India for a portion of the commercial and, lo and behold, American Express okayed the idea. Conan would need some staff to go with him. But with Conan's head writer, Mike Sweeney, and his executive producer, Jeff Ross, both in deep preparations for the new show, the only option left was me. So, Conan asked if I wanted to go to India with him to help him out as he shot the commercial for American Express. Of course, I happily agreed.

When I talk about *how* we flew to India, it is by no means a flex. I'm not discussing this as a humblebrag because I'm well aware of the fact that I didn't receive this perk because of anything I did. I also am aware of how obnoxious this is, but because American Express was paying all the expenses for the trip, Conan and I flew to India with first-class tickets through Emirates airline.

Like I said before, I'm economy class. I am used to paying for every little item on a plane—extra chips, a carry-on bag, alcohol, headphones, everything. So when my Montebello, California–born ass casually walked onto Emirates first class, I was entering a whole new world.

There aren't too many seats in first class because they cost an exorbitant amount of money (someone told me they're $25,000 per ticket, but that hasn't been confirmed). Plus, they're not even seats; they're FOUR-WALLED SUITES. Yes, four walls. You sit down and close the door, and you are encased by four walls. When it is time to sleep, they turn off the lights, light fake stars on the ceiling of the first-class cabin, and send you off to a sweet, first-class sleep.

Halfway through the flight, I woke up because I was hot and realized no one could see me, so I did what any normal person would do and I took my pants off. On an airplane. The rush! I went back to sleep in my pants-less glory, knowing no one could see me, or judge me, or touch me. During the moments I was awake, I was obnoxiously reclining in my seat, sipping champagne and watching *Glee.* I don't know who I became, what alter ego had assumed control of my body, but I felt like I belonged in first class and never wanted to leave. When we finally got to Dubai fourteen hours later for our connecting flight to Jaipur, I asked if I could stay on the plane.

Eventually, we got to India and we stayed at this incredible hotel that used to be the home of a maharaja. There was a man who would hit two sticks together in the garden to keep the birds away. That was his job.

I know I was there to help Conan and production with whatever they needed, but I got so swept up in the luxury of it all that I became a useless blob. We would go to set, and I would just sit in the shade and eat craft services like a queen. I don't know if I did anything for anyone on that trip, including Conan. I had photo shoots in my room with the silk robe the hotel provided. I would meet Conan for breakfast in the mornings and eat lavish spreads. At night, I would order expensive drinks with my meals. I was a new woman. It was as if American Express had paid for me to go to India and Conan tagged along.

I had a boyfriend at the time and we were still pretty new when I went to India, so I would try to Skype him from time to time. At one point, I went shopping and I bought him a sitar. When we flew back to LA, I put the sitar in one of the empty first-class suites. This trip was a year and a half into working for Conan, and I realized that I could and would change at a moment's notice—that there was a person inside me who had no humility when confronted with the decadent things in life. Conan would've been better off not taking anyone with him at all. If I provided anything, it was fodder for riffs. At one point, Conan was looking out the window of the plane and I had my champagne in my hand watching TV and Conan told me to come look at the Russian topography. I was so deep into *Glee* that I told him I'd look at it later. He loves telling people I would rather watch *Glee* than look at Russian topography. If I gave him anything, it was that story. That's it.

Business trips are a big part of any job that requires them. They're a chance to showcase to your colleagues how you act outside the office, and most people don't allow their lack of professionalism to be seen by anyone they work with, especially their boss. That day, when I was sipping champagne and watching TV in my personal Emirates suite, I showed Conan my true self: someone who flies coach and clearly can't handle the opulence that is afforded to her by riding on his coattails. I shoved professionalism aside and decided to take

HOW TO NAP AT WORK

1: When choosing furniture for your boss's office, go couch shopping with him. It will not only establish you as a pleasant companion for small tasks, but you can test out some couches for nap time.

2: You don't want a couch that's too hard so you can comfortably nap. You also don't want something that's too soft in case you get overly comfortable and your hour-long power nap becomes a two-hour-long power nap.

NAP AT WORK (cont.)

3: Now that we've chosen the right couch, we have to be strategic about the placement. Do you put it where it can easily be seen from the door? Of course not! Find a way to move it to a more discreet location.

Success!

NAP AT WORK (cont.)

4: Spend the next few months studying various footsteps. Once you've identified your boss's gait, you can put this knowledge to use and eliminate the last hurdle to Naptown—your boss.

5: Remember, you are the keeper of his schedule. Decide when you want to nap, then set a meeting for him as far away from you as possible.

6: Almost there.

7: Walk into his office.

NAP AT WORK (cont.)

8: Check the area for stoolies.

9: Nap.

the opportunity to make myself comfortable. Rather than pretend this side of me doesn't exist, I decided to lean in. What I felt was similar to how in one of the Tobey Maguire *Spider-Man* movies, Peter Parker lets Venom take over his body and becomes drunk with the power he feels. It becomes an all-consuming change in his demeanor, his appearance, and his overall attitude. I'm Peter Parker, and the perks I get from my job are Venom. I don't remember the movie, but I'm sure it turned out great for Peter.

Our Trip to UCSD

In the spring of 2012, the *Hollywood Reporter* decided to do a cover story on Conan. The reporter, Stacey Wilson Hunt, is a longtime entertainment journalist and an all-around wonderful person. As part of the story, Stacey came with us to the University of California, San Diego campus to watch as they honored Conan by temporarily naming one of the colleges on campus the "Conan O'Brien College."

UCSD comprises several different undergraduate colleges. I guess it would be a little like Hogwarts, although I never read the Harry Potter books or watched the movies, so I'm only going off what I think Hogwarts is like. So maybe it's not the best analogy. I wouldn't know. Anyway, there are seven undergraduate colleges at UCSD. Students get to choose which college coincides best with their personality and objectives in college. As a celebration for their tenth anniversary, the students at one of the colleges renamed it Conan O'Brien College for the day.

To commemorate that, Conan, a couple of our staffers from the digital team, our publicist Drew Shane, Stacey, and I all took the train down to San Diego for the event. We stayed at a nearby hotel for the night, and we were going to head back the following morning.

When we got to UCSD, we had a long day of meet and greets with students, tours of the campus, and finally a Q&A that a student conducted with Conan in front of an audience of thousands of UCSD students and faculty. It was a great day.

When we got back to the hotel, I took a marijuana edible to unwind and get ready for bed. Right after I took the edible, I noticed a text from Drew saying everyone was going to dinner at the hotel. Did I allow taking an edible to deter me from a free meal? Of course not. Should I have? Yes.

I'm not a stoner by any means. I don't wake and bake. I'm rarely, if ever, high at work. But at the end of a long day, give me an edible and let me stream *Parks and Recreation*, and I'm transported to my happy place. And this had been a long day.

I met everyone for dinner at the hotel restaurant, and for the first forty minutes I was normal. I was engaged in the conversation as Stacey casually asked Conan about the day, learning more about his process and digging into his interaction with fans for the story she was writing. Everyone was on their A game because a cover story for the *Hollywood Reporter* is a big deal. It was one of the few pieces of press Conan had done post-NBC. This was one of the times I knew to be professional. I didn't engage unless I had something important to add, I didn't make any crude jokes, I stuck to one drink so I didn't get belligerent, and when I did join the conversation, I tried to be thoughtful. And I was doing great until forty minutes into the conversation. That's when my edible kicked in. I slowly morphed from a professional member of a team into a high college student.

I started laughing at things that weren't that funny. When Conan or anyone else made a slightly amusing comment, I laughed loudly. Or I snickered in a way someone who is high would snicker in order to mask how high they were. When I spoke, I would start sentences and forget the point I was trying to make halfway through. Everyone would look at me in order to be polite, then, confused, look away as I trailed off. And then there was the food. I not only shoved everything that was on my plate into my eager face, but also took my fork and started digging into Drew's leftovers. We had already eaten the complete meal in the first forty minutes, when I was sober, but after I got high, I started ordering more food. Tuna tartare, French fries, hummus dip. My palate was all over the place. When no one else would eat the appetizers I ordered, I would say something like "I don't want all this food to go to waste," as if I was doing everyone a favor by jamming it all down my throat. I ordered dessert and lots of water. So much water. Too much water. And when my glass was empty, I would say things like "I need water" or "Is anyone else thirsty?" When the server came by the table, I would desperately ask for more water, then, five minutes after getting it, ask for more just as urgently. You know when someone is drinking so much water that they barely breathe, then when they stop drinking they're out of breath because they were drinking too quickly? That was me and my cotton mouth. It was as if I had taken Ecstasy instead of an edible.

All this in front of a journalist for the *Hollywood Reporter*. Conan noticed what was happening to me and decided to dig in. He wasn't upset, because Stacey seemed amused by it all, so he started purposely asking me questions to embarrass me and put me on the spot.

"Sona, what did you think of the event today?"

"I thought it was really cool the way the students . . . how they would interact and, um, I'm sorry, what?"

"The event today. What did you think?"

"Oh, I thought it was great."

"That's it?"

"No, I liked the way they got excited and how they would, uh, sit and listen and, um . . ."

[Silence for five seconds]

"And what?"

"What?"

"You said the way they sat and listened, and it sounded like you were going to say more."

"Did I? No, that was it."

"Are you sure?"

"Sure about what?"

"Are you sure you had nothing else to add?"

"Add to what?"

"To what you were saying about the event today."

"Oh yeah, it was great."

"That's it?"

[Server comes by] "Can I please have some more water? I'm so thirsty."

"Should I just bring you a pitcher of water?"

[This server is a dick.]

"Why are you drinking so much water?" Conan asks, amused.

"I like water."

"It just seems like you're drinking a lot."

"Does it?"

"Yeah. More than usual."

"No, I think I'm drinking the normal amount. I don't know why you're getting on my case about hydration."

"I'm not getting on your case. I just think you're drinking more water than you normally do. It's just odd."

"What's odd?"

This happened several times throughout the night—Conan passive-aggressively letting me know he knew I was high without ever addressing it outright. He knew I was hanging on by a thread, and he lives for these moments.

The restaurant was outdoors, and they provided blankets to the customers because it would get a bit chilly at night. I took a blanket, wrapped myself up in it like a burrito, and then fell into a full REM cycle right at the table. I might have even snored.

I had some drool on my face.

Years, and I mean *years*, after that dinner in San Diego,

Conan would find ways to let the fact that I was high at a dinner with a reporter casually work itself into conversations with someone, anyone—to let them know that, despite how I behaved, the article came out great. And I learned to ask if there were any dinner plans before I left for my room during a work trip.

Men

I was single throughout most of my time working for Conan. I had a few short-lived relationships, but for the most part, I was actively single. Like so many people do with friends at work, I would tell Conan all about my dating adventures, and sometimes introduce my dates to him. When we were grabbing drinks at a bar and I noticed someone, Conan would act as a wingman. I quickly learned: Conan is a terrible wingman. This might be surprising considering how Conan talks about me to reporters, HR, and his audiences, but it's not that he didn't talk me up like you'd want a wingman to talk you up. He did, actually. It's that anytime anyone found out I worked for Conan O'Brien, they only wanted to talk about him. When they realized I was at said bar *with* Conan O'Brien, they only wanted to talk *to* him. And most of the time, they continued talking to me just to get within his orbit. In that way, Conan was the ultimate cockblock, achieving the absolute opposite of what he set out to do. But bless his heart, he tried to help me as best he could. It's just that sometimes I was beyond help.

UNLESS OTHERWISE CREDITED, ALL PHOTOS ARE COURTESY OF THE AUTHOR

Here I am happily posing with a prop of Conan's head. This was from a shoot for Conan's cameo in *Sharktopus vs. Pteracuda*. In the movie he gets mauled by a sharktopus, and nearby beachgoers play volleyball with his severed head. MEGHAN SINCLAIR/TEAM COCO

Conan went into makeup for two hours to look like the character Melisandre from *Game of Thrones*. We shot this for a cold open for one of our shows at Comic-Con. MEGHAN SINCLAIR/TEAM COCO

My brother, Danny, wanted to work in finance for as long as I can remember. He must've been around ten in this photo we shot on a normal day at home with my parents, grandparents, and great-grandmother.

I was told I could invite some family to the screening of the Armenia episode. They regretted that decision when they saw how many members of my family I brought. RUTHIE WYATT/TEAM COCO

For a bit on our show, I spent an entire week bingeing as many episodes of *Friends* as I could. After I was done, I visited shooting locations on the Warner Bros. lot. Here I am in front of the fountain the show used for the opening credits.

I got to travel to Jaipur, India, for Conan's American Express commercial shoot. It was the fanciest way I've ever traveled.

One of the first pieces of comedy I was featured in for the show involved Conan hunting down my lost mug, which was merchandise from the show *Gigolos*. A couple years later, I got to meet one of my favorite gigolos, Brace, when I was on a trip with friends in Las Vegas.

Conan and me during an appearance on the show.

TIFFANY ROOHANI/TEAM COCO

After dinner my friends and I found this police car sitting in front of our studio and took it around the lot for a joyride.

We shot an entire comedy segment where Conan tore down my car. A few months after we shot that segment, my car stopped working while I was driving on a busy Los Angeles freeway. I had it towed to the nearest CarMax and took photos with it before I got rid of it.

In that same segment, Conan bought this awful car for $500 and presented it to me on the air. Until today, people ask me if Conan bought me a nice car, thinking he presented me with this car on the show then gave me a nice car off-air. As generous as Conan is, he would never do anything that would take away from the bit, and buying me a nice car off-air would take away from the bit. CHRIS MILLARD/TEAM COCO

Sometimes when we're interviewing incredible people like Michelle Obama or Catherine O'Hara and Eugene Levy, I zone out and have a voice in my head that keeps telling me how much cooler they are than me and I forget to pay attention to anything they're saying. AARON BLEYAERT/TEAM COCO (ABOVE) · TEAM COCO (BELOW)

Conan and Liza at my wedding. ANI STUDIO

At many Armenian weddings, guests throw money into the air on the dance floor. While Conan was dancing, people were throwing money on him, which he would then pick up and dance with. ANI STUDIO

Conan and me at lunch two months before I gave birth. ANI STUDIO

When Conan hosted the White House Correspondents' dinner, we got access to the White House grounds to take a tour of the press briefing room. This is me posing in front of the White House during a very "How Did I Get Here" moment.

I was asked to be a guest on the show to fill in for Kumail Nanjiani, who had to cancel his appearance at the last minute due to scheduling conflicts with *Silicon Valley*. It was a thrill to get to sit in between these two guys.

TIFFANY ROOHANI/TEAM COCO

Conan and me lounging near a pool in Cuba in between shooting for the first *Conan Without Borders* episode. JASON CHILLEMI

Me posing with my speech trophies.

How I would fight off a Conan zombie in a zombie apocalypse.
MEGHAN SINCLAIR/TEAM COCO

When we were doing a week of shows in Atlanta, we were invited to the Carter Center where I got to meet former president Jimmy Carter and First Lady Rosalynn Carter.

A shot of me and my very messy desk at *The Tonight Show*. I could never keep a clean work area.

Conan and I drove to the middle of nowhere in the mountains of Armenia to shoot a segment where we're herding sheep. Here we are sitting in a small Soviet car we both thought we were going to die in. AARON BLEYAERT/TEAM COCO

When Conan and I were in Armenia, we shepherded sheep in the mountains in traditional clothing. For obvious reasons, no one dresses like this anymore.

JESSIE GASKELL

Me, Conan, and our field producer Jason Chillemi at Largo. During the COVID pandemic, we were shooting our shows out of the venue in West Hollywood with a skeleton crew of twelve people. I was very pregnant with my twin boys. MARK FLANAGAN

A photo of Conan with a paper mustache. My father has a mustache, and sometimes Conan would make mustaches out of things like paper or napkins and we'd take a photo and send it to my dad.

Conan and I were bunkmates on the tour bus during the Legally Prohibited from Being Funny on Television Tour.

Conan played HORSE with Magic Johnson and I got to meet him during the shoot. Conan lost. TEAM COCO

I had a chance to ride on a Rose Parade float in 2016. We did a bit on a show where I brought Conan coffee while riding a makeshift float in the studio. Here I am waving to the crowd after having made fun of Conan to the audience. MEGHAN SINCLAIR/TEAM COCO

Underwear

I went out on the four worst dates of my life with the same person. Wait, first, a note. I'm not going to give any details about this man because he is a human with feelings, and he probably doesn't realize how terrible he is. I'll keep the details vague so he has a chance of a future with another woman.

We met while playing a recreational sport in Hollywood. Everyone would go to a bar after the games and socialize. I always noticed him and thought he was cute, and on one particular day, he asked me to hang out. He lived not too far from the bar and told me to come by after. He said we would grab some food or go somewhere for a drink, and I said sure. He left before me, and after a little bit I went to his apartment.

When I got there, he answered the door annoyed. He apparently had begun playing a video game when he got home from the bar and became engrossed in it. I had interrupted his flow. Good start. He told me I could wait for him to finish playing this one section and then we could hang out, and I, again, said sure. He took me to his room, where there was an elaborate computer setup complete with a comfortable gaming chair. Next to this monstrous setup, there was a small, uncomfortable stool, which I came to realize would be my seat.

So I sat down on this stool and thought maybe I'd watch him play and he would explain it all to me. Not my dream date, but hey, I could go with the flow. That's not what happened. He promptly sat down and put on noise-canceling headphones with a microphone. I sat there watching him play a game I didn't understand without hearing a thing that was happening. He would talk to other players through the microphone, and to be fair, it sounded exciting. I just sat there, smiling like an asshole, pretending to enjoy myself, just happy to be involved.

I thought it would take about ten minutes for him to finish this thing he needed to finish, but forty-five minutes came and went and I was still sitting in this man's filthy room, on this uncomfortable stool, watching my prospective suitor play a video game I didn't understand and couldn't listen to, all while being ignored.

It took me longer than I'd like to admit, but I eventually worked up the courage to get up, wave at him for his attention, then politely mouth "I'm leaving." He glanced over at me, waved goodbye, and went back to his game.

The following day, I went to work and told Conan all about it. He listened to the story like a real pal. I know it's odd to think about someone sharing a story about a botched date with their boss, especially when that boss is a celebrity. But he's the person I work with most closely, and my personal life inevitably would seep into my work life. Also, Conan was genuinely invested. HE's been happily married to Liza for almost twenty years, and I think he enjoys dishing about other relationships. He loves to give advice on dating and he's good at it, so I figured I would get his advice on this guy. Yes, I was still considering dating him. Being completely ignored during an impromptu date and still considering going out with him shows you how low my standards were. Sometimes I felt as though as long as a guy had a pulse I would go out with him. Conan laughed when I recounted the gaming adventure I'd had with this guy and asked if I would see him again. Conan always held his reservations about the men I dated—I think he thought that if he said something mean about them, it could come back to haunt him if I ever married one of these people.

When I saw the guy again at the bar the following week, he didn't apologize about what had happened at his house; he just came up to me like everything was cool and asked me out again. I, being insecure and pathetic, agreed.

The second date, he planned something for us to do. We were going to have dinner and see a movie. So I drove to his house and picked him up (he didn't have a license or a car . . . in Los Angeles). He told me he had already purchased tickets for the movie, and he asked if I was cool buying dinner, to which I replied sure. He got in my car and gave me directions for where to go to get food and I thought about how nice it was that he had actually put in some effort for this date. I had misjudged him. I thought about how good it was going to feel to tell Conan this story of redemption—how this guy started off as such a dud but took the second date as an opportunity to show me his worth by choosing a movie and a place to eat without needing my input. It was refreshing to know someone had thought of all the details without needing my intervention. I felt vindicated.

Until I realized the place he had chosen for dinner was 7-Eleven.

Let me explain.

Actually, there's nothing to explain.

The place he chose for the two of us to grab dinner was 7-Eleven. As in your local neighborhood convenience store. It's the place you go to when you're stoned at 3 a.m. and need some Doritos. That's where this guy took me. For dinner. On a date.

He went aisle by aisle grabbing food as if he was grocery shopping at a Ralphs. At one point, I told him I was happy to buy snacks from the concession stand at the movie theater. He said it was too expensive there, as if he were paying for it. I shrugged and grabbed some Rolos.

When we got to the cashier to pay for the snacks, he said we didn't need a bag, then promptly grabbed everything he had gotten and shoved it all into my purse. I had a big tote bag at the time and didn't realize how handy it would be for smuggling snacks into a movie theater. I guess I hadn't foreseen the date going quite like this.

We got to the movies, and as soon as the lights went down, he asked for his food. All of it. He had gotten a hot dog, a cheeseburger, some taquitos, heated up a burrito, and finished it off with chicken wings. It was all smelly. Thank goodness! I had been beginning to worry it wasn't embarrassing enough. I thought no one would notice we'd brought in food, but thankfully it stank up the whole theater. The entire row in front of us kept turning around and giving us the stink eye. Meanwhile, this douchebag I was on a date with was gleefully eating his 7-Eleven food. I pulled out my Rolos and ate them, making sure everyone saw that *I* wasn't the source of the smell; the guy beside me was. It felt like the smell lingered in the theater for the next two hours. It was the longest movie of my life.

Again, I found myself recounting the date to Conan. Again, he listened and nodded his head. I could tell he wanted to say something, but he was biting his tongue. Conan gave me a sympathetic ear, like a reliable gal pal. He listened, he didn't judge, he told me I should do what makes me happy but to make sure I didn't settle for anything less than I deserved. Segment producers would be waiting outside his office to discuss that day's show guests, and I would be wasting Conan's time talking about a turd of a man who forced me to be one half of the smelly-food duo in a movie theater. Meanwhile, I was emphatically saying I would never go out with this guy again and how embarrassed I was and how I felt like I was regressing.

Which is why it was even more disappointing when I agreed to go on a third date with him.

Don't judge me. Actually . . . yes. You can judge me. I should be judged. I don't even know why I agreed to go out with him again. I think I was bored. Either way, we made plans to grab something to eat.

On the day of the date, I remember texting him to ask if we were still on for our date. He told me we were and that he was going to take a quick nap and I should text him when I left my house. So I got dolled up—wore a cute dress, did my hair and makeup, shaved. You know, the things most people do when they're getting ready to go out on a date.

I texted him when I left my house.

He told me to text him when I exited the freeway.

I texted him when I exited the freeway.

He told me to text him when I got to his house (please remember that this man didn't have a license or a car).

I texted him when I was standing outside his door and again after I rang the bell a few times and got no response.

He answered the door in his underwear.

I'm going to say that again: he answered the door wearing nothing but his underwear.

He seemed annoyed I was there, much like the first time we hung out. I clearly had woken him up from his nap. I now understood that every time I texted him, he would try to maximize his nap time by asking me for regular updates of my journey to his house. I stood there at his doorstep in my cute outfit with my hair and makeup done in front of a guy in his underwear with blanket lines still imprinted on his stupid face. He then said (in an irritated way), "I'm napping. You can come in if you want," then disappeared back into his apartment.

I stood there knowing this was a moment of reckoning. I could hold on to whatever dignity I had left and leave, or I could forfeit all self-worth and follow him inside. I stood there thinking about it for a long time. I had always given too much of myself to men who made very little to no effort, and it was time for me to grow out of that phase. I needed to understand that I was worthy of something more and that I didn't have to settle for being mistreated time and time again. This guy was one of a long line of men who behaved this way—who did the bare minimum, trusting that I wouldn't object. I always let them get away with it. I really needed to break the cycle.

But not this time.

I followed him inside. I hate myself.

I went to his room, where he had already gotten back into bed. His room was filthy. Not messy, but filthy. There were plates that had crusted-up old food still on them, glasses that looked like whatever beverage was inside had evaporated long before, clothes strewn all over the place. I had to walk over things to get to his bed, and when I got to his bed, I just took off my shoes and weirdly lay there next to him. After some time, he made a move, and it was painfully awkward. He went in for the kiss and I wasn't expecting it so I flinched and hit his face with my hand. Then, when we started to kiss, there was absolutely nothing there. I felt nothing. Maybe a little disgust. It was the first time I understood what people meant when they said they had no physical chemistry with someone. After clumsily trying to get the mood going, I had to stop it. He was in his underwear, his breath smelled like he had been napping for hours, his room was a disaster zone, and I just couldn't handle it anymore. I got up and said, "I have never seen anyone try so little." He laughed. I left.

When I told Conan about this date, he couldn't hold it in anymore. I think the guy answering the door in his underwear took him over the edge. He had never heard of something so disrespectful, and as my friend, he was horrified for me. He also thought it was hilarious. He finally took the opportunity to tell me what I needed to hear, which was that I was worth so much more than this guy—that I needed to realize I deserved more instead of settling for whatever nonsense this was. He wanted me to truly understand how awful this guy was and how I shouldn't settle for so little. He was right. He also wanted to make sure I knew this story was going to be brought up for many years after as a bit. He's a great sounding board, but he's also a comedian, and I had given him a great gift—the gift of material that never gets old.

"How bad is Sona's dating life? The last guy she dated didn't even bother getting dressed for the date. He probably couldn't get a ride to the mall to buy some clothes."

This has been my curse since working for Conan. If anything embarrassing happens to me, I know he'll make fun of me for it for a long time after. The frustrating part of all this is I also know I *have* to tell him. I feel compelled to. And it can be anything—guys I was dating, superstitions my family followed, stories about me going out with my friends.

The time I was dancing on a table at a bar and I lost my balance and fell off? Not pertinent to work, but I told Conan anyway. The jokes came fast and furious.

The time I dated a guy who forgot my name in the middle of the date? Again, not pertinent to my job, and I knew it would be material for Conan to make fun of me, but I told him regardless.

Anyway, let's not get off track. By now, you're probably thinking the underwear date would've taken me over the edge, right? That there's no way I would ever agree to go out with this guy again. But as I said in the beginning of this section,

I went on the FOUR worst dates with this person, so if you're counting, you already know I went out with him again. Only this time I loathed him. When I got his text asking me out, I genuinely couldn't believe his nerve. I stopped thinking about how he could redeem himself and went only in the same way someone would go near a house fire to watch it burn. I wanted to see how bad it could get. Would there be any remains below the scorched surface? Some shred of humanity? Some semblance of a guy who actually liked someone and wanted to try to really put in the effort this time? And WHY this guy wanted to go out with me after our incredibly awkward make-out attempt was beyond me.

As much as I didn't understand why I kept agreeing to go out with him, I also couldn't understand why he kept asking me out. I was becoming more and more vocal about how awful he was, so why was he coming back for more?

This time I was going into it fully aware of the reality, knowing that I was no longer looking for anything redemptive and only engaging with him to see how badly he could ruin things further. Was this a slightly self-destructive dating strategy? Perhaps. But I couldn't look away from this train wreck.

Again, he had purchased tickets for a movie showing nearby, and again, he asked if I'd be willing to pay for the dinner since he got the tickets. Sure, I said. I was never one of those women who expected the man to pick up the whole tab. It's nice when they do—don't get me wrong—but it's not a deal-breaker for me when they don't. This time, instead of going to 7-Eleven, we went to a restaurant. And it was definitely not a 7-Eleven. I'm talking tablecloths. I'm talking wine lists. I'm talking a goddamn maître d'. The movie tickets couldn't have been more than $15 each, so when the bill for our meal came and it was $150, I knew I had gotten the short end of the stick. Whether he was overcompensating for the 7-Eleven taquitos, or whether he was just hoping to squeeze a nice free meal out of a doomed situation, I'll never know. I just paid the bill but made a mental note for future retellings.

We started driving to the theater, and when we were just a few minutes away, he asked if I could turn around and go back to his apartment. It turned out that he had forgotten his joint at home and he hadn't watched a movie without getting high first in over ten years. It was imperative, according to him, that I waste time and gas and turn back to his house to get this joint, and like an idiot, I did it. During dinner, he had been so busy shoving a free three-course meal into his mouth that we didn't really get to talk, so the car ride was when we had a chance to get to know each other a bit better. You might be thinking, "I'm sure once you actually got to know him, there was something about him you liked." You would be wrong.

He told me he worked as a production assistant for a total of one week out of the month. Because his apartment was rent-controlled, that's all he needed to work to cover his monthly expenses. The rest of his time was spent getting high with his roommates and playing video games. This grown man approaching thirty told me all this as if it were a selling point. Like he was a genius for hacking the system. I didn't judge him to his face because I'm not heartless. And truly, whatever works for you. I just added a new mental note and delighted as the story got better.

We went to the movie, which was surprisingly great, and then I drove him home. We sat in the car for a while when we got back, and I just laid it out for him. I told him how we shouldn't go out anymore because he wasn't putting in the same effort I was and how I felt like I was being taken advantage of. I told him I didn't appreciate the way he would invite me over, then act annoyed once I got there. I recounted our previous three dates and told him I needed more and that it was partly my fault because I had been letting him get away with it without telling him I didn't like the way he was behaving. He seemed confused and tried to defend himself.

"I was playing that game when you came over and only needed a little bit more time to finish what I started! You don't want to date a guy who starts something and doesn't finish, do you?"

"I thought I was saving you a lot of money by going to 7-Eleven instead of getting food from the concession stand at the movies!"

"I woke up really early that day for work and wanted to nap to be fresh for our date!"

Gaslighting bullshit. I wanted to punch him.

Finally, I just said, "I need to stop dating guys like you."

It came out worse than I meant it, or maybe it came out exactly as harsh as I wanted it to? I think I wanted it to be that mean. I'm not sure. Either way, the point hit the mark. He got out of the car and went home. I didn't think he cared, which was the hardest for me to reconcile—that this guy behaved the way he did because he didn't *actually* like me.

I told Conan everything that had happened, and he breathed a sigh of relief. He and I both knew I would never go out with this guy again, so Conan finally let it out. I would love to say this was an isolated incident, that it was the only time I misjudged a man I dated and made a bad decision. But it was not. This man was one of many men I dated who I let get away with treating me like hot garbage. Conan met many of these guys and always let me figure it out for myself. He knew *telling* me these guys weren't worth it wouldn't be enough. I would need to come to that conclusion myself. Because of that, I kept going back to him for advice. "What should I text this guy that just texted me a smiley face?" "How eager should I sound about going on another date with this guy?" "Do you think it's a red flag that he's been unemployed for two years?" "How bad is it that I've never seen him sober?" These are all questions I've asked Conan about the men I've dated. These are the conversations that have held up the flow of the day. I've ignored important phone calls because I was too busy gabbing with my pal about boys, as if we were in the nail salon getting mani-pedis and not in a professional work environment that relies on proper timing to produce a television show. Anyway, Conan made jokes about the guy answering the door in his underwear for many years after that. When people asked me about my dating life, he happily recounted the stories from this one guy, illustrating how terrible my judgment was with men. And he was right—I was a disaster.

That was until, of course, I met my husband. When I first told Conan about Tak, he knew it was different. He could tell this one was for real, that he was someone who was going to woo me properly, that he was going to put in the effort Conan thought I deserved.

Five years later, Conan and Liza would be at my wedding.

Two years after that, I welcomed my two sons into the world. Two boys who I can raise to know better than to answer the door for a date wearing nothing but their underwear.

My *Gigolos* Mug

On June 25, 2013, I went to the kitchen to get my daily cup of Earl Grey tea in the morning. I used a mug that my friend Meghan Sinclair had given me for Christmas—a piece of merchandise from the show *Gigolos* that said "Gigolos" on one side and "Working Stiff" on the other.

Gigolos was a show my friends and I were all fascinated with. It followed the crazy antics of five or six men who were gigolos in Las Vegas. Women would hire them for company and, oftentimes, sex. It was soft-core pornography with a very vague plot. So it was just soft-core pornography. We loved Brace, who could've been either forty-five or sixty-five years old, for his unfiltered comments to his clients. Vin was known for having a large penis. Bradley was the new guy who had a military past. My favorite, however, was Nick Hawk, who had a massive tattoo that originated from his penis and eventually spread over his entire body. I still follow him on Twitter.

When I went to get my mug from the kitchen on that warm June morning, it was missing. People think that because a mug is in the kitchen, it's there for everyone to use. But no. You cannot use a mug for a TV show if you don't watch it and IT'S MY MUG. It happens often, though. Someone sees a mug in a communal space and assumes it's a communal mug.

This time when my mug went missing, however, I snapped. I wrote an email to the entire staff. I used a company-wide email address that goes to every staffer, crew member, and Turner employee affiliated with our show. The email address was used only for production purposes or important messages, and I felt the email was necessary for my missing mug. I wrote:

> I know this is a complete misuse of "Hey Everybody" but if you stole my Gigolos mug I'm going to find you and destroy you.

I got varying replies from several different colleagues, some commending me for finally speaking out against the theft that occurs in the office on a regular basis, some laughing at what they thought was a joke email, and some asking what "Gigolos" was. None of the responses told me where my mug had gone.

An hour after I sent the email, Conan came to my desk with a camera crew.

They were there, he said, to investigate the matter further. He interviewed other staffers in the office to find out what had happened to my mug.

Lindsay Sheehan, who worked near me at the time, complained that people drank from the bottle of whiskey that was stashed in her desk.

Keri O'Keeffe, the talent coordinator, complained that someone once stole a pair of her headphones.

John Bogulski, the assistant to segment producers, was eating fried chicken at his desk and seemed annoyed when Conan came by to interview him.

Eventually the mug was found—an intern had delivered it to my friend RJ Thieneman, who works at Conaco. Not only had the mystery been solved, but we also had unearthed much more workplace dirt through Conan's investigation:

- People drink at the office all the time. I was just as upset as Lindsay when I found out someone drank out of her whiskey bottle, because that wasn't just her stash—it belonged to all of us.

- People steal other people's belongings at work constantly. This was the first instance of theft I had experienced at work, but I feel like my hardship had given a way for a lot of other people on staff to talk about their trauma.

- Unlike on many other shows with a famous host where people cower anytime the boss is around, no one is afraid of Conan.

- As a team, we are willing to waste time and office resources on literally anything, including a full-scale, filmed investigation into a missing *Gigolos* mug.

Our office is full of criminals and drunks. Something about Conan's investigation resonated with people, and as of the moment I'm typing this, the video has racked up almost twenty-six million views on YouTube.

That video was my first notable appearance on the show and the first glimpse of my relationship with Conan in the office. People had seen our interactions in the *Conan O'Brien Can't Stop* documentary, but this was a look into how we spoke to each other in a professional setting. It was also the only piece we shot that my parents were not too excited to watch. Something about your daughter using a mug from a television show featuring soft-core pornography is not something you want to brag to your friends about, apparently. That wasn't the only *Gigolos* paraphernalia I had at the office either. I had magnets on the refrigerator of all six original gigolos from the first season. No one would ever take my magnets.

But I digress.

After I sent the initial email about my missing mug, Matt O'Brien, one of our writers (who would eventually become a head writer of our show), sent me this email in response:

What a sad window into your life

A sad window indeed. This wasn't the first time someone used my mug, but it would be the last. These petty office squabbles are what I live for.

After that bit aired, Showtime sent me twelve *Gigolos* mugs, and two years later, I would have the distinct honor of meeting Brace from *Gigolos* in Las Vegas. Ironically, I was in Las Vegas with Matt O'Brien's wife, Meghan Sinclair, and Matt was the one who set up the meeting. Brace was really sweet and we chatted for over an hour. I did not have to pay him. Dreams do come true.

PART THREE

Producer Tracy King calls Sona to tell her they are ready for Conan in rehearsal. Sona pops into Conan's office to tell him. As she goes in, he asks her about her progress.

CONAN: Any luck with that thing I asked you?

He's being vague on purpose. He knows she forgot. What an asshole.

SONA: Yeah, it was no problem at all.

Sona hates lying to Conan and rarely ever does, but her cockiness is getting the best of her.

CONAN: Really? I know people who are having trouble with it. It's highly anticipated and everyone wants to get their hands on it.

SONA: Yeah, but I'm really good at what I do and people like me, so it was easy.

CONAN: Where is it?

SONA: It's on its way now.

CONAN: Thanks, Sona. I think you really understand how much this means to me and I'm proud of you for getting it done so quickly.

Wow. Fuck this guy.

SONA: Of course. I'm happy to do it.

Conan leaves for rehearsal and Sona sits at her desk. Guilt washes over her, and she sits there thinking about everything Conan could've possibly asked her.

Okay, let's think of the things he's interested in:

The Beatles! She googles "The Beatles" and a billion different results come up. She stares at the screen. She then googles "New Beatles thing." Another billion results come up. This isn't working.

Gadgets! Maybe he asked her for some new gadget. But why would any gadget mean anything to him? He orders them, plays around with them for a while, then either gets frustrated or finds something else to focus on.

Buddy Holly? Is there a guitar or new memorabilia or a book?

A book! That sounds familiar. He asked for a book.

What book? What does he like? Murder! Is there a new murder book? Would a murder book "mean a lot to him"? She googles "new books on murder," and as she looks at the results, she realizes nothing pops out at her.

Okay, we know it's a book. If it's not a book on murder, then it's a book on history. American history? World history? Ugh, why does he read so much? How much knowledge does one person need?

She googles "new historical nonfiction books," and there it is. It punches her in the face—a New York Times *article on the new Robert Caro book. The book he's been working on for ten years, meticulously researching his subject in an effort to write an opus that is as in-depth as any historical book can be.*

She calls the booker on the show who books authors and asks her how hard it would be to get the unpublished manuscript.

THE BOOKER: I can ask, but some of the offices on the East Coast are already closed, and even if they are open, they won't be able to send it here until next week since FedEx is already closed.

The next two hours are spent calling everyone she knows—taking frequent snack and bathroom breaks in between calls, obviously. The breaks are longer than the phone calls. Everyone in publishing on the East Coast who can help her is already out for the day. If she'd just started earlier, she probably could have gotten this done pretty easily. She can't catch a break, and she can't help feeling like this might be the reckoning she deserves. She should've written it down. She should've come clean with Conan and asked him what it was he wanted. This will be worse than him being angry at her—he'll be disappointed. She blew it.

AUTHORITY

AUTHORITY IS AN INTERESTING CONCEPT IN CONAN'S AND my dynamic. He's the boss, the one who signs my paychecks, the one who hired me, and the one who I'm ultimately supposed to make sure is happy. My entire role revolves around doing what he needs me to do in order to make sure his life is easier. I am his assistant, after all. I assist him on things he needs assistance with.

But at times, I do the opposite. I talk back to him a lot, I forget to put things in his calendar, I annoy him with my flippant disregard for things he feels are important. I don't know how the relationship evolved in terms of how I respect authority, but it did.

I've always had a complicated relationship with authority figures. In school, I would often socialize with my friends instead of paying attention to my teachers, resulting in many trips to the vice principal's office. One teacher would get so irritated with my inability to pay attention that he made me sit outside of the class and copy the text in the science book word for word. I was often in detention and Saturday school. One time, the teacher tasked with sitting with the students in Saturday school got so upset at how I corrected his pronunciation of my best friend's last name that he kicked me out. There's nowhere to go after Saturday school except suspension, but my offense wasn't bad enough for suspension, so I just went home. It's not that I was an asshole—in fact, long after I graduated school, many of the teachers who reprimanded me would speak of me fondly. I just couldn't stand being told what to do.

I respected authority until I became more familiar at work. It's not that I stopped seeing my bosses as authority figures—it's that with my new level of comfort, I didn't feel that level of adulation was still important.

One of the biggest arguments Conan and I had was a result of how I came to view a changing dynamic between us—how Conan went from being an authority figure to my friend and surrogate brother. In the time since, I've learned how to navigate that and have realized that our job is to work toward a common goal. I'm there to make sure the host of the show has what he needs and is where he's supposed to be when he's supposed to be there. We don't need to have a typical boss-assistant relationship to make that happen; we just need to make it happen.

But I've come to respect that he's my boss. Even if he sometimes acts like my child.

The End of Conan's *Tonight Show*

I had worked for Conan for almost a year when he got word that there were going to be changes in the late-night lineup and that the network was considering putting Jay Leno back in the 11:35 p.m. slot. Jay had embarked on an ill-advised 10 p.m. show that tanked, and because of his contract, NBC realized it would be more cost-efficient to keep him on the air, so he'd have a half-hour show on at 11:35 p.m., which was coincidentally the same time as *The Tonight Show. The Tonight Show with Conan O'Brien* would be pushed to a start time of 12:05 a.m., removing the literal meaning of "tonight" from *The Tonight Show.*

What followed after was the most inspiring, emotional, frustrating, and educational moment in my career.

Inspiring because of the massive support Conan and the show got from his fans. Conan's fan base has always been ardent, and they showed up when we all needed them the most. I had known he was beloved before I started working for him, but I didn't realize how beloved until this moment.

Emotional because no one knew what was going to happen. So many of my colleagues on the show had moved their entire lives from New York to California to work on a show that now faced uncertainty. We were also overwhelmed with the love we were getting not just from the fans, but from allies at the network and the press.

It was a frustrating time because I had worked for the publicity department at the network before I started working for Conan, and I suspected they were the source of so much misleading information that came out in the press. It was jarring to think some of the people I used to work with might now be the people who were trying to disparage my new boss with planted stories and anonymous quotes.

This time was educational because, up until this moment, I had been shielded from the ugliness of television. I never truly saw the ruthless underbelly that existed below the flowery surface—the underbelly that I knew was there but naively believed I would never have to see. I saw people I would work with on a daily basis take sides. I also came to think that Jay Leno might not be the nice guy I'd thought he was. The man who always boasted about not having an agent or manager was now teaching me how important it was to have an agent or manager. I couldn't believe how quiet the man who had hosted *The Tonight Show* for seventeen years seemed to be about the show being moved a half hour later. Didn't he also think it was a terrible idea? Or was he so desperate to get the show back that he would stop at nothing for the time slot? I didn't know what to think anymore. All I knew was that I was disappointed.

But I tried to focus on the positives. Some would think my favorite memory from this time was the support from our fan base, or the inspired writing on the show those last two weeks, or the outpouring of support from some big names who made the end of *The Tonight Show with Conan O'Brien* so memorable.

But my favorite moments have nothing to do with any of that. When Conan's name was thrust even more into the spotlight, the press wanted any glimpse of him outside the studio, so they started waiting for him down the street from his house.

He didn't love all the attention, especially at a time when there was so much uncertainty around his career, so he asked me to give him a ride to work. Why me? Easy. Because no one would believe he, Conan O'Brien, would drive around LA in a white 2007 Volkswagen Jetta. He was right. For two weeks, I drove from Pasadena to Brentwood, picked up Conan, and drove us both to work. Not a single member of the paparazzi knew where he went. We would drive straight through the throngs of photographers, and I'd park in his spot at the studio like a baller, with him crouching down in the backseat so no one would see him.

My other favorite moment happened very late in the evening when we were all waiting for Conan's exit contract with NBC to be ready to sign.

Conan's office was on one side of the hallway, and Jeff Ross's office was on the other. In between there was a conference room that was usually for meetings, but during those two weeks it was being used as a war room by an army of well-dressed attorneys who were negotiating with NBC around the clock.

The night after his final show, Conan was in his office with me and Rick Rosen, his longtime agent. We were waiting for the contract to be done, and it was tense, to say the least.

We had nothing to do, so we started flipping through the channels, and we stumbled upon what was one of my favorite shows at the time—*Bad Girls Club.*

Bad Girls Club was a show on Oxygen that explored the lives of women who were . . . to put it delicately . . . very easily triggered. The show took seven women and made them live in a house together, and then filmed everything that happened. It was *The Real World* with seven women with tempers and apparently healthy libidos. They fought, they hooked up with strangers and with each other, and they partied hard. If I could have an alter ego, it would be a Bad Girl from the *Bad Girls Club*.

I exploited Conan's vulnerable moment and used it as an opportunity to catch up with this insane reality show I watched at the time. Conan, Rick, and I sat there without speaking. Conan and Rick were contemplating the next career move for Conan. I was contemplating how the Saddle Ranch on Sunset Boulevard was just as trashy then as it was when my friends and I had gone there five years earlier. Together, we watched these seven women fight each other and hook up with strangers for hours, until a lawyer walked into Conan's office and told him it was time. The lawyer presented the exit contract for Conan to sign, and just like that, Conan ended his time with the network he had been a part of for over sixteen years.

To this day, I can't watch *Bad Girls Club* without thinking of that night—waiting with his powerful agent for a pivotal moment in my boss's career to transpire while watching seven women fight each other at a nightclub in Hollywood.

In that moment, I could've encouraged some reflection or, better yet, I could've left Rick and Conan alone. There was so much on their minds, and I'm sure it didn't help that I sat in between the two of them and made them watch a show that had the opposite of a calming effect. I could've done better, but I don't regret a second. I freaking love that show.

Meeting Presidents

Before I wrote a book called *The World's Worst Assistant*, I always thought the title of my memoir would be "What Am I Doing Here?" I've asked myself that question a million times throughout my years working for Conan. When I'm at the Emmys—what am I doing here? When I'm flying in a private jet during Conan's 2010 tour—what am I doing here? When I'm eating snacks backstage at Comic-Con—what am I doing here?

It's not because I don't think I've earned the right to be there, but more because I long ago had resigned myself to the idea that I simply didn't belong. Let me explain.

I grew up in the Los Angeles suburbs, graduated from a public school, and then went to a community college, from which I eventually transferred to USC. My father came from humble means—a child of two orphans, he was one of six kids and grew up in a village in Turkey. He immigrated to the US when he was a teenager and became the general manager of a lunch truck catering warehouse in downtown Los Angeles. My mother is from Istanbul—her father was a butcher from the time he was twelve. My mom immigrated to the US when she was in her very early twenties, married my dad about six months after coming here, and raised my brother and me full-time. Why am I telling you this? Because my exposure and access to the opaque world of Hollywood and television is a fluke. My job working for Conan is a fluke. I still don't know how I got this job, and there are moments when I'm doing something really cool, like sitting across from Bill Burr while Conan is conducting an interview with him for his podcast, when I am forced to ask myself, genuinely, "What am I doing here?"

I'm not the daughter of someone famous. I didn't go to one of LA's prestigious private schools. Most of the friends I grew up with don't even work in the entertainment business. To have experienced the things I've had the joy of experiencing is and always will be monumentally exciting. When we did a Zoom interview with Ted Danson for the podcast, I lost my mind even though it was virtual. It was VIRTUAL. I remember leaving the Zoom when it all ended and texting everyone I thought would care.

But nothing has ever gotten me as starstruck as the times when I met former presidents Bill Clinton and Jimmy Carter. It has nothing to do with my political beliefs and everything to do with what it represents. I'm the granddaughter of genocide survivors, and here I am rubbing elbows with two men who for a time were the most powerful men in the world.

Jimmy Carter

I met Jimmy Carter and Rosalynn Carter when we were preparing to do a week of shows in Atlanta. The Carter Center is in Georgia, and I honestly don't know how the meeting was arranged, but somehow, I got looped into an email chain with Jimmy Carter's office to coordinate a meeting with Conan and the former president. Conan knows more about presidential history than anyone I know and always jumps at the opportunity to meet a former president, so off we were.

The plan was for only Conan to meet President Carter in his office, so I escorted him there and introduced myself to President Carter's assistants and then took a tour of the center by myself.

I saw a replica of President Carter's Oval Office and so many relics from his time in office. I walked around like a tourist, killing time alone and learning about history. I got why Conan was fascinated with presidential history. I've been to the Reagan Library and to the Lincoln Library, and they're all so different. "I should read a book on American history," I thought. Then I laughed as I realized I never would.

It was a lovely place and I had a nice time. Then, after about an hour, I returned to the office where I'd dropped Conan off. While I was there waiting for Conan to be done with his meeting, one of President Carter's assistants asked if I'd like to meet the former president. I was shell-shocked.

"Me? Are you sure that would be okay?"

"Yes, of course!" It turns out Jimmy Carter is a very cool guy.

When I walked into the office, I was speechless. I took one look at the Carters and froze. Then I did what I always do when I'm overwhelmed, which is cry. I *cried*. It wasn't a weepy type of crying, though. It was an eyes-welling-up-and-voice-cracking type of cry, and I'm pretty sure I said something like "I can't believe I'm meeting you." He was clearly touched. He offered to take a photo with me and told me I could stand next to him. It's like I was a teenager again at a Justin Bieber meet and greet and it was 2011.

Standing there in that office in Georgia with a former president and his First Lady, I was overwhelmed with joy. I remember first getting my job and having someone tell me never to get jaded, and this was one of those moments when that popped into my head. It's easy to get used to the "what am I doing here?" moments. It's easy to get into a mindset that you have always lived that lifestyle and forget that ten years earlier you were waiting for seven hours in the standby line at Tower Records on Sunset so you could meet George Michael and never did because once he got through the line of people who had wristbands he couldn't get to the standby line because of time constraints and it stung even more because you were second in the standby line and you could peer into the store and see everyone having a nice moment with him.

Anyway, getting to experience some of the things I've experienced will never get old and I'll never get used to it. I think of this moment every time I see Jimmy Carter in the news, building a house with his bare hands or beating cancer in his nineties, and remember how welcoming he was to me, even though he didn't need to be. It reminds me that you can often be blown away by how kind some people can be even though they've experienced the highest points of notoriety. I've been lucky to meet and work with people like that, and although fame can get old, human greatness never does.

Bill Clinton

In 2016, Conan moderated a panel with Bill and Chelsea Clinton for the Clinton Foundation. Even watching from backstage was a big deal for me. I was thrilled to have been even a small part of planning this event. It was their annual Clinton Global Initiative University, where college students from all over the country came for a weekend of networking and workshops. It was a fantastic event, and this was the closer for the weekend.

Conan did this great Q&A with President Clinton and Chelsea, and afterward we all found ourselves outside the auditorium where the Q&A had taken place. When I looked behind us, I noticed a line of people who were clearly getting ready to meet the former president. I was standing there with Conan; the head of our digital department, Steve Beslow; and one of our bookers, Britt Kahn. We stood there as Clinton made his way to us and started talking to Conan. Steve, Britt, and I kept moving out of the way so the two of them could have their privacy, and the former president kept moving with us to include us in the conversation. It was an awkward circular dance with multiple people involved, like a very slow human tornado.

Clinton's time in office was problematic and ultimately the scandal that got him impeached was disappointing to those who supported him, but he was still a president for two terms and, again, my joy at being in a position where I could meet someone that influential wasn't lost on me. Also, President Clinton was in office while I was alive. I remembered his presidency and that made him a larger-than-life character for me. He wasn't a person but a caricature—a saxophone-playing, lower-lip-biting Southern charmer. That moment in that hallway after the onstage Q&A, he became a human being to me.

HOW TO ABUSE YOUR CORPORATE CARD WITHOUT TECHNICALLY EMBEZZLING

1: Acquire said credit card.

2: Start small.

3: Then start pushing the limits.

4: Always bring up work somehow so you can justify the expense as work related.

5. If Accounting gets suspicious, 'fess up to something small and offer to correct the mistake.

6. Lay low for a while.

7. Then start small...

8. Repeat cycle.

I have no idea what he said, though. My thought process went something like this:

"Oh my God, he was the PRESIDENT. I wonder what it's like to live in the White House. If I lived in the White House, I'd have parties every week. I wonder if you can invite anyone you want to come hang out with you when you live there. What is he talking about? Why did he just say 'irrigation'? Should I be paying attention to him? What if he asks me a question? Oh no, he'll realize I'm an absolute idiot and I'll have to make something up and hope it fits into the conversation. I wonder what Arkansas is like. Is there an actual little rock in Little Rock? Where did it get its name from? Is he the most famous person from there? I mean, who else would be more famous than a former president? It's like Nixon being from Whittier, I guess. I can't believe a president is from a town that is so close to where I grew up. Why am I thinking about Nixon when Bill Clinton is right in front of me? I wonder if Hillary is ever going to run for president again. I'm sure she'll do great."

And so on.

Before I knew it, we were in a circle gabbing with the former president for what must've been at least twenty-five minutes. The long line of people he had to meet behind us was getting visibly anxious. Eventually, someone from Clinton's camp came in and broke up the conversation so he could move on to everyone else. I really wish I'd paid attention to what he'd had to say.

Gender

I chose a profession that has a very problematic history with sexual boundaries. I came into it fully naive, and eventually when I encountered a woman who I thought was unfit to work in a certain position, I assumed she had slept her way to the top. I was unabashed about it—completely unapologetic about my assumptions about certain women. I was a part of the problem until the #MeToo movement blew up and I had a reckoning that the way some women are treated in the entertainment industry is more than gross; it's abusive and criminal. I'm shocked that until then, I had chalked up the way some men spoke to me as part of me "paying my dues." I needed to be harassed to move up. How dumb. Here are some stories about the times I came to a harsh realization about my role as a woman in the entertainment industry and how it shaped my image of authority.

A Lesson in Gender Roles

I made it a point to have an internship every semester in college. When I first started school, I wasn't sure if I wanted to work in movies or TV. After interning at a film production company, I learned that the movie industry moves too slow for me and I preferred the almost instant gratification that television gives. In the movie world, there's preproduction that takes forever, then shooting that takes forever, then postproduction that takes forever, and then what you're left with are these two hours of film. I'm sure I left out a ton of steps, but I don't work in movies, so who cares.

On the other hand, you could shoot a TV episode in one week and it could be on the air the next, or, in the case of late-night TV, the day of. What a thrill. Anyway, that's not relevant at all to this topic. What is relevant is that in one of my earlier film production internships, I got a harsh lesson in gender roles in the entertainment industry.

I was nineteen and had gotten an internship at an independent film production company in Los Angeles. It was a small company, so they gave the interns a good amount of responsibility. At one point, one of the assistants in the company gave me a script written by the daughter of one of the producers of *Rocky.* He said to read it and give him notes, which I did. I wasn't crazy about it and neither was he, so he told me to call the person who wrote it and tell her we were passing on the script. I didn't understand why I would be the one making that call. It felt like too big of a job for an intern, even considering the extra responsibility. At the time, I didn't know that "passing" on a script meant we're not moving forward, so I called her and told her we were passing the script on, which has a completely different meaning.

"You're passing the script on?" she asked.

"Yes."

"Oh my God! So one of the producers is going to read it?"

Me, completely befuddled and confused: "Yes."

"This is so great!" You could practically hear the champagne bottle popping in the background.

Me, sweating: "Okay, so someone will call you. I've gotta go."

I knew there had to have been a mistake. The assistant and

I had talked about the issues with the script, so why would he want me to call this woman and tell her we were passing the script on? Also, who were we passing the script on *to*? Why didn't I ask that question when he told me to make the call? And finally, WHY WAS I MAKING THAT CALL? I was a nineteen-year-old who had been working in the entertainment business for five minutes. I wasn't even paid. I didn't know why the assistant had me calling this person and telling her if we would be moving on with her project. How was that my job? Couldn't I just make a coffee run?

I went back to the assistant and I told him what had happened with the call. He looked visibly frustrated. Fuck this guy. Again, WHY WAS I MAKING THAT CALL? To make matters worse, he made *me* call her back and explain the misunderstanding. What complete hell I was living in that day.

I called the woman back and give her the bad news. That I had misunderstood their assessment of the script and that I misspoke. I never told her I was an intern who didn't understand the business, which was the sole reason I was doing an internship in the first place. Seriously, no one wanted coffee? I might as well have been negotiating contracts.

She was understandably upset, and we hung up and I wanted to climb into a hole.

Okay, so I'm realizing this story has little relevance to this topic, but I'm already rolling, so bear with me.

A couple months go by, and at that point I'm in comfortably with everyone in the company. It's small and I've been given a fair amount of responsibility (clearly!), so I'm feeling good about myself. One of the producers in the company asks me if I can help him sort scripts in his office, an opportunity I jump on. I'm eager to ask anyone who is willing to listen a million questions, and I think, what better time to pick someone's brain than when we're sorting scripts?

Before I can even ask if it's okay for me to ask him questions, he says, "Now would be a good time for you to ask me whatever you want to ask."

Giddily, "How did you get started producing movies?" Generic. Easy.

He answers.

"Is this what you always wanted to do?" Again, generic. Easy. I'm throwing softballs here. It's how the entire conversation goes. Who's his mentor? What did he study in college? Uninspired questions getting canned responses. Until my last question, which is when I ask him if he has any advice for me.

"Women in this industry only move up if they work ten times harder than men or if they're insanely attractive."

Well . . . shit.

Even though I was hungry at that age, I was aware of who I was. I was never going to work ten times harder than anyone. I was going to put in an adequate amount of effort and then cross my fingers that my charisma would propel me the rest of the way forward. Even if I were the type of person who might be able to pull that off, I don't even know how you would quantify working ten times harder than a man. Do you take how many hours he is working and multiply his hours by ten and work that many hours in a week? What if he works forty hours? There are way less than four hundred hours in a week, so how would I even do that? And when would I sleep? I love sleeping. Or maybe I take a male colleague's effort and just multiply that by ten? How? How do you multiply effort? If he takes a half hour to pick up lunch for the office, how would I do that ten times quicker? Can I physically pick up lunch in three minutes? If a male colleague is good at answering phones, how can I be ten times better? Should I be ten times more cheerful? Ten times more accommodating? If I answered the phone and he never did, how would I even know what to base my effort on? This all sounded like I was being set up for failure.

As for my looks, I've always been happy with my appearance, but I know I'm not "insanely attractive." My parents and my husband are probably the only people who would say I'm that good-looking, but my mom thinks, genuinely believes, that my brother looks like Jon Hamm, so can we really trust her judgment? She also thinks I have a great singing voice, which is even more damning evidence of her mom bias. Unfortunately, neither my parents nor my husband run an entertainment company, so what good does it do me anyway if they think I'm pretty? It wouldn't help me get ahead in Hollywood, apparently.

This is the idea I had of the entertainment industry when I was nineteen—that I was doomed for failure because this one producer arbitrarily set rules on what a woman would have to do in order to succeed in this business.

I recently googled him to see what he was up to, and he hasn't produced a movie in almost fifteen years. Maybe he should try working ten times harder than the other producers. Or being insanely attractive.

My Ass

It was a typical day in the office. Conan hadn't yet gone down to the studio for rehearsal and he was taking his morning meetings. I was toggling between the Netflix window and my Outlook window, multitasking like a champ. I got up to grab a snack from the kitchen, and that's when it happened.

In order to get to the kitchen from where I sat, you would have to walk through the main lobby of the floor. Our office coordinator sat there and would check people in for meetings. Our office coordinator was also in charge of the interns, so there would always be interns milling around waiting to be given instructions for runs.

At this point in my time working for Conan, I had already been in a few taped pieces on the show, so viewers of our show were beginning to recognize me. As I was walking to the kitchen, a man in the lobby who looked to be waiting for a meeting with one of our producers saw me and called out to me.

"Sona!"

I turned around and saw an older man smiling and waving at me. I couldn't say how old he was, but he gave the vibe that back when he first started working in the entertainment industry it was totally okay to bang your assistant and do lines of coke off your desk. He was wearing comfortable clothes and had his white hair slicked back.

"Hi!"

[I said this to him enthusiastically. I never know how to react.]

"Big fan."

"I'm happy to hear that. Thanks."

"Sona Movsesian—that's Armenian, right?"

"Yes, it is. Like Cher."

"Or like the Kardashians."

"Yup."

[I fake-smile when I talk to people like this. It hurts my face.]

"You don't like the Kardashians?"

"No, I have nothing against them. I just like Cher more."

"Is it because you're jealous of Kim?"

"What? No, not at all."

"Good, because you have a much better ass than she does."

[I stood there silent for a while. I had my fake smile still plastered across my face. I didn't know what else to do but stand there and smile. Finally, after what seemed like forever—]

"Haha, that's definitely not true. I have to go to the kitchen now."

This was offensive on several levels.

First of all, I absolutely do not have a better ass than Kim Kardashian. I've seen her ass in person and it's majestic. She came on the show once with her sisters, and she was wearing a tight black-and-white dress. Another time she came on wearing a tight brown skirt. Both times her ass was accentuated, and it was perfect, so I feel qualified to comment. My ass is not big and it's not small. It's just average. It's not toned, there's a lot of cellulite, it lacks any type of definition. Don't get me wrong, it's not a terrible ass. It's just not as good as Kim Kardashian's, let alone *better* than hers.

Second, this dickhead said this in front of the office coordinator and a couple interns who happened to be in the lobby at the time. This was such an embarrassing way to get undermined in front of my coworker—having an older man remark on my ass. Having anyone remark on your ass is absolutely not okay, but having someone, a stranger even, who looks like they're staring death in the face, is even creepier. I think the worst part about it is knowing how vocal this younger generation of interns is and how I just stood there like an asshole and didn't say anything. There was no "How dare you speak to me like that" or "Don't ever say anything about my ass." Just a meek response. And I just know everyone looked at my butt when he said what he said, thinking they'd see something that would give Kim Kardashian a run for her money, but no. Nothing. Just a poor, pathetic excuse for an ass. So not only did this jerk-off diminish my worth down to just a body part, he belittled me using a body part I'm not even proud of. If he'd commented on my boobs, that would have been another story.

And finally, I WAS AT WORK, getting a snack like I always do. He ruined snack time for me and that is unforgivable. As I walked into the kitchen, I felt disgusting, like someone had stripped me naked in front of everyone at work and grabbed a pointer and directed it to my ass. I was angry the interns saw that interaction and even angrier that they saw me take his comment quietly.

After leaving the kitchen, I walked into our area where Conan and Jeff Ross's offices are, and I was recounting the interaction to Jeff's assistant. Conan heard and came out and asked me what had happened, and so I told him. He was playing his guitar and I saw the gears turning in his mind. Then he looked at me and said, "What do you need me to do? I don't know who he's having a meeting with, but I'm happy to tell him to leave." I almost cried. It was a Tale of Two Men—one making a woman feel like garbage and the other using his position to stand up for her. If anything, the interaction made me realize I was working for the right person, even in an industry that has a long way to go. While there is still a contingent of people who are stuck in the past, a new wave of progressive men and women is making it difficult for the old guard to thrive anymore.

I looked at Conan and told him he didn't need to worry about it. "That douche is going to die soon anyway" is what I actually said. Then, after the meeting the guy had with one of our producers, I walked into that producer's office and told him what that guy had said, hoping the revelation would deter the producer from inviting the man back in to the office (which it did). Was it going to help this old man learn the error of his ways? Not at all. But I felt good about it nonetheless.

Don't Date Coworkers

When I was an intern at a small TV production company, one of the assistants asked me out. I was a sophomore in college at the time and I knew it was a bad idea for me to go out with him, but I said yes because he was cute and I thought it would be awkward if I rejected him. I thought a good compromise was for him to go out with me and my friends to a concert we were going to at the Roxy that weekend.

We met up at the Roxy and went to the concert, then we all went to grab drinks afterward at a bar nearby on Sunset Boulevard, then finally we grabbed some late-night food.

There were about five of us in the group, and it became very evident early on that this guy from work was a dud. Sure, he was good-looking, but he didn't have much to talk about, he didn't have a sense of humor, and anytime he did say something, it didn't add much to the conversation. It would just kind of hang there. After we ate, he walked me to my car and I successfully rebuffed his advances, knowing that going to my internship on Monday was going to be very awkward.

And it was.

There was an interoffice messaging service we used between employees, and he messaged me as soon as I got to my desk just saying hi and opening the door for a flirty conversation. He sat a few feet from me, so he could literally see my facial expressions when I read his messages. I offered no smile, no look of longing. Just stoicism, which is always a bad sign. For the sake of the internship, I realized I had to be honest with him and tell him I wasn't interested. Well, not completely honest—I told him we couldn't keep dating because we worked together. A flimsy excuse when you've already gone on a date. But I dutifully typed out the message and sent it via office IM.

Of course, my ego wanted to believe he'd be devastated, that he'd plead with me to reconsider. But he didn't. He barely even flinched. Then he asked me if one of my friends who had been with us when we went out was single because he wanted her number. You can't fault a guy for trying. But then he didn't ask me to do anything for him or his boss throughout the rest of my time interning at the company. He barely acknowledged my existence. I would message him asking if he needed anything and he'd just respond with "no thanks" or "all good." Right.

So that's how I learned it was a mistake to date someone at work. If it didn't work out and I was honest with them, I still could get iced out. My internship was great, but it could've been even better had I been given the opportunity to help everyone in the office without worrying about a fragile assistant getting in the way. I took that realization with me to every job after that—relationships are messy, and so complicating work relationships with romantic ones can only hinder what you get out of a job.

And no, my friend wasn't into it. Poor guy got rejected twice.

Dave

In May of 2015, I got a call from David Letterman's assistant, Mary Barclay, giving me a heads-up that a gift was being delivered to Conan. That year, Conan had penned a lovely tribute to David Letterman for Dave's final show. As a thank-you, Dave got him a gift.

She called me to let me know it would be a difficult delivery. She made it clear that it wasn't a typical gift and that it would require special attention and the lot would need to be notified. I was intrigued. I told the head of our security, Jim Stack, that something was being delivered and I wasn't sure what it was.

We get things messengered to us all the time, and it's never been a big deal. The messengers or parcels get screened at an off-lot location, then get brought to the studio. I couldn't imagine what was going to be so difficult.

Later, the security booth at the entrance called me, concerned.

"Do you know there's a delivery for Conan?"

"Yes, thanks. You can just have the driver come to the studio."

"It's not going to be that easy."

"It's not? Why?"

"We'll talk to Jim."

A little while later Jim called my desk.

"It's a horse."

"What's a horse?"

"The delivery that came for Conan. It's a horse."

"A real one?"

"Yes."

"I don't understand."

"Someone delivered a horse to the lot for Conan."

"What do we do with it?"

"We're working on getting it onto the lot right now."

"Okay."

I walked into Conan's office. I didn't want to tell him what it was and ruin the surprise, so I just said there was a delivery from David Letterman and he had to go outside to get it. Confused, Conan went out of the studio, walked down to the small alley by the side of the building, and there it was: Conan's comedy hero had sent him a horse as a thank-you gift. A big eleven-year-old brown-and-white horse named Dave.

We all stood there, baffled. No one had any clue what to do next, so Conan did the only thing he could do. He got on the horse and took a photo. After a few minutes of looking at the horse and petting it, we all realized we had to figure out what to do with it after the show. In the meantime, Dave the horse went back to the ranch from where he came, waiting to see what the horse's new family would do with it next.

I won't discuss what this meant to Conan or what later became of the horse because it's not my story to tell. What I love about this is how Mary, Dave's assistant, had to arrange everything. It's what the job of an assistant is—if your boss says "send Conan a horse," you have to figure out how to do it.

In June of 2009, Michael Jackson died. I was about six months into my time working for Conan, so our rapport was still being established. Conan always gives me a call to check in when he's on his way into the office. After we went through the usual business, he said he had a request.

"Oh, one last thing—I know Michael Jackson died recently and I want to be able to say goodbye to him the proper way. Can you call Drew [Shane, our publicist at the time] and see how I can have a private viewing of his body?"

"Yes, of course," I said emphatically. I didn't know what Conan's relationship was with Michael Jackson. What if they were friends? Six months wasn't long enough for me to know who Conan did and didn't have a relationship with, so how would I have known the request wasn't legitimate? To add insult to injury, I dutifully made a note in my notebook.

Call Drew—private viewing of Michael Jackson's body for Conan. Time alone to say goodbye.

As with a lot of requests, especially ones from my early days, I didn't know how I was going to do it. I just knew it had to get done. So, my gears started turning trying to figure out who I would get in touch with to arrange for Conan to have some alone time with Michael Jackson's body. I knew these requests were going to happen as soon as I started working for a celebrity. I knew there were going to be moments when I was going to get a request unlike any I'd ever had before. I had watched the movies and I had spoken to enough assistants to know that sometimes our bosses were going to ask for odd things and we were just going to have to get it done somehow.

Conan and I ended our conversation and I started brainstorming. Do I get in touch with someone from Michael Jackson's team directly, or should I go through Drew? Do you go through publicists to handle a request this personal? If Conan was close to Michael, maybe he was also close to the other Jacksons. Would it be weird for me to find a way to contact Janet? Why wasn't there any contact information for Michael in Conan's address book? Maybe it was under an alias? I didn't want to bother Conan with any questions about this, but I might have to since it was so personal. If I was going to spend time with a friend's body to say goodbye, wouldn't it be more appropriate to go through less professional avenues?

While I was thinking about my next step, Conan called me again. He went through a few more show-related things he needed me to get done, then threw this in there at the end:

"I just thought of something—call Leigh Brecheen [Conan's lawyer] and ask her what I would need to do to adopt Blanket."

"Michael Jackson's son?"

"Yes," he said, amused by himself. Over the years I would come to understand what the inflections in his speech mean—when he is doing a bit and when he is serious. He would never be able to get away with this kind of request now.

"Is this a bit?"

And that's when he started laughing. He asked, "Did you think I was serious about the private viewing of his body, too?"

I didn't respond. I let him have his moment.

A few minutes later he walked into the office and started telling everyone the story. Then he looked at my notebook.

Call Drew—private viewing of Michael Jackson's body for Conan. Time alone to say goodbye.

There it was—evidence that I had taken him seriously. He took my notebook and started showing everyone he could find. It was brutal. That was a big learning moment for me—not only is most of what Conan says a bit, but he also loves when he can take something I do and make everyone laugh at me. I realized that while assistant duties like running errands or keeping his schedule are valuable to him, being fodder for his riffs is an even bigger gift. Perhaps what has kept me employed all these years has been that I'm an endless well of material, and although I may lack in other areas, that's far more valuable for him.

Throughout my time working for Conan, I learned that he's not the kind of guy to ask for things that are impossible to figure out. Getting reservations at a popular restaurant, or tickets to a sold-out show, or a product that is no longer available is actually easy for me to do for him because so many people know who he is and love him. Nine times out of ten, anything that Conan needs to get done will get done without any heavy lifting. Every once in a while, we do encounter

THE ART OF EXTERNAL CONVERSATION

Master essential reactions. During conversations, identify the feedback your boss is looking to get. Execute the appropriate facial and verbal response, then confidently check out.

1. ADMIRATION

2. CONCERN

EXTERNAL CONVO (cont.)

3. OUTRAGE

4. SYMPATHY

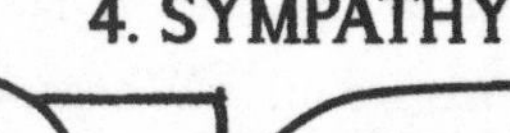

people who don't know who he is, and those are some of my favorite moments. They bring him back down to earth.

This one time after we shot a remote at the Santa Anita racetrack, we went to a popular dumpling house called Din Tai Fung in a shopping plaza nearby (since then it has expanded to a popular restaurant chain, but the original location in the United States was this one, in a small strip mall in Arcadia, California). I told Conan before we went that there was always a long wait at this restaurant because it's so popular, and he boastfully said he would take care of it. He confidently walked up to the hostess and asked for a table for the three of us. The hostess looked at him blankly and told him it would be a forty-five-minute wait. Our head writer, Matt O'Brien, and I were so happy we were there for that moment. We stood there for forty-five minutes waiting for a table, and every once in a while, a fan would notice Conan and he would take photos with them outside. So many of them asked him why he was waiting, and he had no response. What was he supposed to say? "They didn't recognize me"? What joy.

When we finally did sit down, a few of the employees either googled him or just deduced that he was famous by the response others were giving him, and he started taking photos with everybody. By the end of the meal, he was a celebrity again, but oh, what a forty-five minutes it was.

Anyway, the point is that anything Conan needs to get done can normally get done easily. I'm just glad I didn't call any of Michael Jackson's reps before Conan called me back. I don't know how I would've recovered from that.

Murder

Like I mentioned earlier on in the book, I read *Helter Skelter* while I was working in a watch store in the mall during the early years of college. The story fascinated me, especially as a lifelong Angeleno, though to be fair, LA is a dream for anyone intrigued by murder. You can drive by a town house in Laurel Canyon where four people were beaten to death with pipes, dubbed the Wonderland murders. There's the Los Feliz murder house, where a man killed his wife, then attacked his daughter with a hammer before he killed himself by drinking poison. The house where Marvin Gaye's father shot him is still standing, and so is the condo where Nicole Simpson and Ron Goldman were murdered.

Conan and I found out early on that we shared a common interest in murder when he told me he was reading *Helter Skelter*. I told him I had read it years prior and then we excitedly started talking about these gruesome murders. I think I was only a few months into working for him, and I was excited we had found common ground already, even if it was the shared fascination with the brutality of murder.

One day, Conan had a shoot after the show, and we had to stay late. He had sent his car back earlier that day, so I was tasked with driving him home. As we were driving, Conan realized we were near Benedict Canyon, the area where members of Charles Manson's cult murdered five people, including a very pregnant Sharon Tate. We decided it would be a good idea to drive by the house on Cielo Drive, just to take a look. You know, like bonding.

We googled the original address of the house and noticed that it had been torn down and the address had been changed to avoid lookie-loos and weirdos who were fascinated by murder, like Conan and me.

The house is situated on a small side street off Benedict Canyon, one without too much traffic. It's easy for a car to be noticed there, so when we were driving to the house, we turned my headlights off. Conan put on a baseball hat so he wouldn't be noticed, and we slowed down to a creeping speed.

So there we were—two individuals in a car at a location where LA's most famous murders happened, at a very late hour in the night driving very slowly with our headlights off, the passenger wearing a hat so as not to be noticed. I'm sure the house has had many random people come to look at it, but how suspicious we looked wasn't lost on me. And that's when it hit me—what if someone called the police and the police came to see Conan O'Brien sitting in front of a famous murder house? What would that TMZ headline be?

Welcome to LA! Conan O'Brien and a Random Woman Stalk Site of Manson Murders in the Middle of the Night

Okay, so I know this isn't something I should harp on, but after working for Conan for a while, I realized I was always going to be some random woman who was with him. If the plane that we were flying in crashed, the headline would be:

**Late-Night Host and Comedy Icon Conan O'Brien
Dies in Plane Crash—A Nation Mourns
(A Random Woman Also Dead)**

If together we somehow discovered the cure for cancer, the headline would be:

**Conan O'Brien Changes the World by Finding Cure
for All Cancer, Saving Millions of Lives.
Oh Yeah, a Random Woman Helped Him.**

If we saved children from a burning bus and I saved thirty kids and he saved none:

**Conan O'Brien Saves the Day! Funny Late-Night Quipster
Can Add Hero to His Résumé as He Saves
an Entire Bus of Children from a Fiery Demise.
Some Piece-of-Shit Random Woman Was Also There.**

Most moments I didn't care that I was a "random woman," and on this night, sitting in my car on a quiet street near Beverly Hills watching my boss go outside to take a look at the driveway that led up to the house where three cold-blooded murderers took the lives of five innocent people and an unborn child, I thought it would be okay with me that no one would recognize me if we got caught. I was a few months into my new job, and I was still getting a feel for who Conan was and what my responsibilities were. I never would've guessed they would include visiting sites where famous deaths occurred. If only that were the end of it.

When we were in Washington, DC, on a work trip, we were driving by Ford's Theatre on the way back to the hotel and Conan made the car stop to show us where Abraham Lincoln was assassinated. He explained where he was shot, where his body was taken after for treatment, and told us the exact time when Lincoln was pronounced dead. The details Conan knows about this assassination would put a Ford's Theatre docent to shame.

When we were in Dallas for a week of shows, we visited Dealey Plaza, where JFK was assassinated, as well as the Sixth Floor Museum, located at the spot where Lee Harvey Oswald fired the fateful shots that ended the life of a beloved president. Naturally, we took a tour. Conan often jumped in with a new bit of information that even this tour guide, whose job it is to know everything about the assassination, didn't know.

When we were in Mexico City shooting a Conan Without Borders travel special, Conan visited the Leon Trotsky Museum—a museum housing the room where a man struck Leon Trotsky in the back of the skull with an alpine climbing axe, effectively killing him. Trotsky would succumb to his injuries a day later, despite initially surviving the blow. Conan bought a keychain there with Trotsky's face on it and still has it hooked to his denim jacket.

Strangely, this is one of my favorite things about Conan.

He's so well versed in history. It's what he studied when he was a student at Harvard, and he's maintained a fascination with it since. He's not someone who can be defined only by his career in television. I think so many celebrities allow what they do to become who they are. I've seen so many people who revel so much in being famous that they don't feel a need to expand on that—to stretch themselves beyond their persona and have interests outside of the entertainment world. Conan is equally as excited to go explore a Civil War battlefield as he would be to interview John Lithgow. Well, that might be a stretch. Conan loves John Lithgow. Anyway, Conan is constantly reading about something and educating himself. That's not me. It's one of the main ways we're different. History is cool and all, but if it doesn't have any steamy sex scenes, then what's the point? On that note, I'm sorry this book doesn't have any steamy sex scenes.

Anyway, the house where the Manson murders occurred was torn down in 1994 and the address has been changed, so to retrace the steps of Tex Watson, Susan Atkins, and Patricia Krenwinkel by climbing an embankment near the gate is no longer possible. But when Conan got back to my car after scouting the location, he said he thought the driveway where Steven Parent tried to leave the property before being shot by Watson was still there. He and I sat in the car and craned our necks and took in the street, morbidly fascinated by what had occurred there forty years earlier. It was odd, but it was also a big bonding moment for us.

In the years to come, I would buy Conan books on famous

murders as birthday or Christmas gifts and send him interesting articles on new, gruesome murders that occurred in present day. It's our cute little thing.

In 2017, my husband, a few friends, and I embarked on an Alaskan cruise. While having dinner on the ship one night, we were interrupted by a message on the intercom overhead asking all security and medical personnel to head to the ninth floor of the ship immediately. We were slightly concerned, but not concerned enough to stop eating the ungodly amount of food in front of us. Plus, the murder mystery show on the ship's social calendar was at the very same time, so one of the theories we had for the mysterious intercom message was that it was somehow tied to the show.

It was not.

The following morning, we were supposed to be sightseeing the beautiful Alaskan fjords, but instead we awoke to find ourselves at port in Juneau. The captain came on the intercom to give us an awful morning message about the change in plans:

"Ladies and gentlemen, this is your captain. I'm sorry to inform you that last night there was a domestic disturbance aboard the ship and a woman from Utah has died. Because we were out at sea, this is a matter for the FBI. We will be at port while they conduct their investigation."

Murder. On a cruise ship.

Shortly after, the social director of the cruise came on the intercom:

"Hi everyone, this is your social director. All activities on our social calendar will continue as planned."

As I made my way to the ship's daily afternoon tea (my favorite activity), I thought about the one guy who would be intrigued by what had happened: Conan. I sat at the table enjoying my usual fare of scones, small sandwiches, and pastries, and I drafted an email to Conan describing the cruise ship murder. I felt like Agatha Christie.

Details eventually emerged about the murder, and my friends and I stayed current with updates as they occurred. A man and woman from Utah had been on the Alaskan cruise with members of their family, including their three daughters. After a night out, they came back to their room, where the woman told the man she wanted a divorce. He snapped and beat her to death. Years later he would plead guilty and receive thirty years in prison. In an unsatisfying ending, rather than serving out his punishment, the man was found dead in his prison cell shortly after his appeal was rejected. No cause of death was released.

I would send any article with an update to Conan, who was both fascinated and horrified by the incident. I wanted to talk it out with someone, to try to find some reasoning behind such an unforgivable act. It was nice to have someone in my life I could posit theories with, talking it out in a way that would make sense of it, or at least make it just a story instead of an actual occurrence.

Conan often jokes about how he thinks he'll be murdered one day. How poetic would it be if I murdered him and some forty years later, a boss and his assistant took a drive to where the murder took place? I feel like this is the only way our story can end. This is my confession.

Why Conan Can't Fire Me

You might be asking yourself why someone who has an assistant who writes a book called *The World's Worst Assistant*, a book in which said assistant fantasizes about one day murdering that someone, would continue to employ said assistant. Easy—you have to make yourself necessary. And not necessary in a way that makes you important to day-to-day tasks in the office—I mean necessary in a way that would instill fear in your boss if he ever decided to fire you. Conan gave me a small opening into his world, and I took that info and made myself indispensable. Here are the reasons why Conan would never be able to fire me—you are welcome to take these tactics and apply them to your workplace.

1. If you have access to their financial and/or personal information, quietly bank it in your memory. I've memorized Conan's social security number, his driver's license number, and all his important credit card numbers. Of course, I would never destroy his credit or steal from him if I were ever fired, but the *possibility* that I could is enough to instill fear.

2. Over the years, I have revealed my true self mostly to Conan. I have gotten very close to his family and friends. When Conan asks me to do something, it can fall through the cracks . . . and the cracks are massive, San Andreas Fault–size cracks. When his family or his friends ask me for a favor, I take care of it quickly and efficiently. My plan is to make everyone who matters to Conan think I'm actually good at my job. The intention here is that if he were to ever fire me, everyone in his life would think he was crazy. "She's so on top of it," they would say. "Why would you ever let someone that hardworking go?" they would ask. I might be fired, but he would be considered crazy. Many of his friends work in the entertainment industry, so a simple email to a few of them acting innocent would be enough to make him look unreasonable and help land me another job.

3. Conan is a bit of a luddite. Over the years, anytime he has needed to download an app or open an account somewhere, I've done it for him. Because of my position, I've had to have access to his email and other accounts. I know all of Conan's passwords. Here's what I would do with the information I have:

» Email: I would put on an out-of-office that was littered with inappropriate language, then change his password so he couldn't fix it right away. Then I would reach out to all his contacts and say something horrible to them that would jeopardize his relationships.

» iTunes: I would download all kinds of porn onto his devices. Then change his password.

» Tesla: I would control his car remotely. Then change his password.

» Again, I'm not a monster. I would never actually do any of this, but again, the *possibility* that I could dangles in the air. And in case he never thought of it before, this section in this book is a reminder that I could.

4. You may be wondering if he could just recover his passwords using his email. Many of his online accounts and apps have my email for password recovery. Even his cell phone is under my name. As far as the online world is concerned, Conan doesn't even exist.

5. Conan has made fun of me in emails. I've been compiling these for our inevitable court case in the future. Here are some samples (these are all 100 percent real).

This first email is from Conan to his good friend Lynette. We were going to New York to do a week of shows, and she had emailed him asking to come to one of the tapings. This was his response (and a good example of his positive reinforcement).

FROM: Conan O'Brien

SENT: Tuesday, October 18, 2016

TO: Lynette C

CC: Sona Movsesian

SUBJECT: COB in NYC

I will be there the first week of November—our first show is Halloween. Not sure what my schedule will be like, but definitely come see a show and I'm sure we will get together. Sona will handle it all—she's almost like an assistant. Hahahahahahahahahahah 😈

The following email is a good example of the nonsense Conan emails me from time to time. I've often joked that 90 percent of the things he tells me are complete and utter nonsense. This is just the tip of the iceberg.

FROM: Conan O'Brien

SENT: Thursday, August 16, 2018

TO: Sona Movsesian

SUBJECT: Schedule

Just landed. Could you get to my house and make me a corncob burrito?

On Aug 16, 2018, Sona Movsesian wrote:

I can call Kim and ask her to leave a La Croix on the counter with some almonds.

On Aug 16, 2018, C. O'Brien wrote:

I'm not kidding. Drive over and bring an Onion Mojito, an eyepatch made of dried apricot, and a portrait of Margaret Thatcher.

Here's another example of the positive reinforcement that keeps me going at this job. In Conan's defense, I did respond like an asshole.

FROM: Conan O'Brien
SENT: Wednesday, December 31, 2014
TO: Sona Movsesian
SUBJECT: Question
I'm in the NYTimes crossword puzzle twice today.

On Dec 31, 2014, Sona Movsesian wrote:
I'm surprised you didn't ask why they didn't have you in there three times.

On Dec 31, 2014, C. O'Brien wrote:
What's a four letter word that starts with D and ends in CK that means "Conan's assistant"?

In the following email exchange, he had asked me to get him something, and it was taking longer than expected to get there. There's an edge here from both of us. This is common.

FROM: Conan O'Brien
SENT: Wednesday, February 6, 2015
TO: Sona Movsesian
SUBJECT: The Mat
Every time I see John he asks if the mat you ordered has arrived yet.

Every time I said as far as I know, it has not. Today he said he sent you an email and that he never heard back. I told him you smoke a lot of pot and he laughed. It was fun.

Where's that mat?

On Feb 6, 2015, Sona Movsesian wrote:
Please tell everyone I get stoned. It's nice when strangers know these things about me.

On Feb 6, 2015, C. O'Brien wrote:
He laughed because he thought I was joking. People don't take me seriously when I say that my assistant gets stoned and watches the Bachelor at work. So you're safe.

This next email was a response to not one, not two, but three different emails I sent out to all of Conan's contacts informing them about his new phone number. On the first email I sent, I accidentally put his old phone number. On the second email, I put the wrong area code, and I finally got it right on the third email. This was Conan's response to one of the replies to the flurry of emails I sent.

FROM: Conan O'Brien
SENT: Tuesday, June 23, 2015
TO: L. Mendoza
SUBJECT: Re: Phone Number

You don't understand, Larry, I taught her English two years ago. She still thinks the office phone is the Devil's Watchdog. When it rains, she eats garlic and gyrates in the parking lot.

This is another one of our dumb email exchanges.

FROM: Conan O'Brien
SENT: Wednesday, April 1, 2015
TO: Sona Movsesian
SUBJECT: Today
Because there are 2 tapings, do you see any reason I can't stroll in a bit later? Maybe email me the seg notes if you have them?

On Apr 1, 2015, Sona Movsesian wrote:
Sure. You can come in when you want. I'll have producers email me the notes and I'll send them to you.

On Apr 1, 2015, C. O'Brien wrote:
Excellent. I will be in at five.

On Apr 1, 2015, Sona Movsesian wrote:
Uhhh, wait. Um, you have to be here before that.

On Apr 1, 2015, C. O'Brien wrote:
Fart.

There's nothing really wrong with the next email exchange. It just further highlights how different Conan and I are. (We filmed a remote years after this exchange where Conan joins my friends and me for a midnight showing of *Magic Mike XXL*.)

FROM: Sona Movsesian

SENT: Friday, September 13, 2012

TO: Conan O'Brien

SUBJECT: Lincoln

The trailer for the movie about Lincoln starring Daniel Day Lewis: http://www.youtube.com/watch?v=qiSAbAuLhqs

On Sep 13, 2012, C. O'Brien wrote:

Thanks. I can't wait to see that. It's my "Magic Mike."

Here's an exchange where, once again, Conan kindly reveals what a valuable employee I am.

FROM: Sona Movsesian

SENT: Thursday, October 16, 2014

TO: Conan O'Brien

SUBJECT: Check out these bikes

They are awesome but will kill you if you ride them in LA traffic.

On Oct 16, 2014, C. O'Brien wrote:

Yup. That may be how I die.

On Oct 16, 2014, Sona Movsesian wrote:

Please don't do that. I'm unemployable.

On Oct 16, 2014, C. O'Brien wrote:

At last we agree on something.

Yes, many of these show a lapse in professionalism by both of us, but because he's my boss, the onus is on him, right? Who sets the tone for professionalism in the workplace if not the boss? Anyway, of course I would never ruin his credit or steal from him or sue him for abuse using these emails as evidence, but the *implication* that I can is always dangling in the air. The chance that I could snap and remotely control his car without him knowing it is not only funny but frightening.

I'm sure he'll one day find a way to remove me from his life, but until then, I'll be sitting at my desk enjoying a movie.

PART FOUR

Sona sits at her desk playing with a pooping-reindeer toy her friend Bill in props gave her as a present. You put brown jelly beans into it and move its tail and it then "poops" out the brown jelly beans. Sona has been beaten. She has no idea how she's going to tell Conan she wasted most of the day either eating or calling her friend with impressions of British royalty and just completely forgot what he asked her to do.

An intern brings in the mail and Sona starts a conversation.

SONA: Do you know anyone in publishing?

AN INTERN: What?

SONA: Publishing. Is your mom or dad friends with someone who works in publishing?

AN INTERN: Oh . . . uh . . . My uncle reads a lot. Does that help?

SONA: No. But it's good he reads.

AN INTERN: Yeah. Do you need anything else?

SONA: No, thank you.

The confused intern scurries off. Sona starts looking through the mail—maybe fan mail will distract Conan? That's it—she'll stroke his ego so he's too preoccupied to notice she didn't get what he needed.

The first letter is from a man in Rhode Island.

Dear Conan,

I saw one of your sketches on YouTube about gravy boat lighthouses. I just think you should know that I work on an actual lighthouse and it's nothing to make jokes about. Just because gravy is served in a gravy boat doesn't mean they need a lighthouse. It's people like you who ruin the image of hardworking people like me who devote our lives to making sure boats know where they're going. Fuck you.

Okay, not off to a good start.

The second letter is from a woman in Nebraska. Ah, the heartland.

Hello Conan,

I'm a junior high English teacher in Norfolk, Nebraska. I was watching your monologue on Tuesday and noticed you erroneously used the term "who" when you should've used the term "whom." Here is a refresher from the website Grammarly for your reference:

Whom should be used to refer to the object of a verb or preposition. When in doubt, try this simple trick: If you can replace the word with "he" or "she," use who. If you can replace it with "him" or "her," use whom.

Who should be used to refer to the subject of a sentence.

Whom should be used to refer to the object of a verb or preposition.

I should hope someone who graduated from Harvard would know the difference, but I understand you aren't the only one who writes your monologue jokes.

Have a lovely day,
A Middle School English Teacher

Is that how to use "whom" and "who"? Sona feels like such a dick for all the times she's used the word "whom" to sound pretentious.

FOCUS!

There are a few more letters, but none flowery enough to distract from the mess Sona has made of today. Conan is expecting the book, and he's going to feel so vindicated when Sona meekly walks into his office to tell him that not only is there no book coming, but also she spent the majority of the day fucking around and completely forgot what it was he wanted in the first place.

As Sona is clearing the fan mail from her desk, she sees a package. She looks at the label and it says "Caro" with a return address in New York. Her stomach drops. She rips the package open and there it is—the advance copy of Robert Caro's book FROM ROBERT CARO HIMSELF. The note attached reads:

Conan,

Since you're such a big fan, I thought you'd like an advance copy of my book.

Take care,

Robert

Sona sits there feeling . . . victorious? No. Not that. Lucky? No, not that either. Vindicated? What? Why vindicated? That's absolutely not it. She just feels . . . happy.

She takes the note and the book and leaves them on Conan's desk.

A short time later, he comes up from taping the show and walks straight into his office. Sona sits there and braces herself, then hears him loudly say, "WHAT?!"

Conan comes out of his office and asks Sona how she did it. How did she contact Robert Caro directly, and how did he send a copy of the unpublished book that day with a note?

This is one of those moments when Sona can either revel in this unwarranted praise or come clean.

SONA: I told you I'm good at what I do and people like me.

She says this with no shame at all.

CONAN: I owe you an apology—I really did

believe for a second that you forgot what I asked you to do and I'm so impressed you got this done.

SONA: Of course. It's my job.

She says this with zero remorse, like a sociopath.

Conan walks away and Sona sits there. An asshole with no conscience.

Only that's not what happened. In the many years Sona has worked for Conan, she has found it very difficult to lie to him. So, this is what really happened:

Conan comes out of his office and asks Sona how she did it. This is one of those moments Sona can either revel in unwarranted praise or come clean.

SONA: I didn't. He had already sent you a copy of the book and it got delivered today. I lied earlier when I said it was on the way. I forgot what you asked me to do and I didn't want to ask you again because I felt like you'd do a bit on how I always forget to do things when you ask me, so I thought I'd just remember eventually, only when I finally did remember, it was too late, and I sat at my desk defeated, and that's when the mail came in and Robert Caro sent you the book and

I did nothing except take it out of the package and put it on your desk and I sat here hoping you wouldn't ask me about it.

Conan stands there and nods. He loves this. What an asshole.

CONAN: So what did you do all day?

SONA: I watched some TV, then visited Erica, and then called her and did my Queen Elizabeth and Prince Philip impressions, and then I went to the kitchen a lot and ate snacks.

CONAN: It sounds like you had a productive day.

SONA: Don't do that.

CONAN: No, really, it sounds like you really got a lot done.

SONA: Okay, cool. So, you're just going to be passive-aggressive. Cool, cool.

CONAN: No, not at all. It takes a lot of work to do the things you did, and I'm so lucky I have such a productive assistant.

SONA: Maybe if you created an environment where I could ask you what you needed without worrying if you were going to do bits.

CONAN: You're right, I shouldn't expect you to write things down like every other assistant in the world.

We go on like this, bickering. Some people walk in to talk to Conan, roll their eyes, and walk straight out as soon as they hear what's going on. This happens often.

STRESS

I'M NOT THE TYPE OF PERSON TO STRESS OUT—I NEVER HAVE been. In sixth grade, my teacher, Mrs. Hackett, said, "There's a solution to every problem," and for some reason that stuck with me so intensely that if there's ever an issue that comes up that can be a source of stress, I brush it off. A solution is out there. Maybe someone will find it.

But there are times when I might brush it off a bit too much.

While I may never stress, it's in Conan's DNA to sweat the smaller stuff. I shrug things off, and he wants to make sure things get done properly. I figure life is too short to care about the mundane details, so why stress over them? He revels in the minutiae.

The only problem is my entire job depends on me paying attention to the mundane details.

When Conan goes to an event, if I don't pay attention to

the small details, then he'll just be walking around confused with no idea what to wear or where to go or when to be there. There will be no car to pick him up, and his luggage will be in a different city. I try to make sure I never leave him in that position.

One of the biggest arguments Conan and I ever had was over an accessory for his new car. He had purchased a car and was told this one accessory would be available later in the year. Months later he ran into a friend of his who also purchased that same car and already had the accessory. Conan asked me about it, wondering why we had never been notified and why I never followed up.

Excuses were made, and it snowballed into a big argument. Of course, he wasn't angry about not having the accessory—he was angry I didn't care that it was available, and that I wasn't on top of it. To add fuel to the fire, I dismissed it, telling him (rather flippantly) that it was just an accessory and that he shouldn't make a big deal about it. I should've just apologized, but here we were, fighting about something small that was indicative of a bigger issue.

That's the problem with my lack of stress—it's inevitable that something will fall through the cracks. And this is where Conan and I butt heads. In the past, I've shrugged it off or given a half-assed "Sorry." I know he wants me to *care* more, I can tell it would make everything between us so much easier, but I JUST CAN'T.

There were times when I was younger when I would lose sleep over letting something fall through the cracks or failing to complete a task properly. But then I grew up. I realized adults make mistakes, and as long as we acknowledge them and move on, then I don't know where the harm lies.

So now I don't stress. I breathe, I set boundaries, and I just live my life. You might be thinking, "Sona, it's a really good thing you're not a surgeon or a pilot." And you are right. People would die.

A Typical Day

You might be wondering what a typical day for me is like. I'm happy to give you an accurate rundown of a regular day for a personal assistant to a celebrity. Oh, the glamour!

10:00 a.m.: Arrive.

10:05 a.m.: Go to the kitchen and make a nice cup of loose-leaf brewed tea and either a bowl of oatmeal or a bagel and cream cheese. Catch up with whoever is also in the kitchen.

10:30 a.m.: Go back to your desk and take time to really enjoy the tea and oatmeal or bagel.

10:45 a.m.: Email a few friends with the subject line "what's for lunch?"

10:45 a.m.–11:15 a.m.: Debate about where you're going to get lunch.

11:15 a.m.: Order lunch.

11:20 a.m.: Figure out who's going to pick up lunch.

11:25 a.m.: Give the intern explicit instructions about what condiments to get with said lunch. (Lunch won't be ready for another fifteen minutes.)

11:30 a.m.: Put in priority parking for said intern so you don't have to wait for lunch once it gets here.

At some point, Conan has arrived at the office, though it's unclear when or how long ago. Maybe he was always here.

11:35 a.m.: Check in with Conan. He asks what's happened so far and you say it's been a pretty chill morning.

12:00 p.m.: Print out the crossword puzzle and sudoku puzzles for the day. You print out the easy, medium, and hard versions of the sudoku puzzle, and if you finish them all, you tell people you completed the "trifecta."

12:15 p.m.: A PA brings the monologue jokes to your desk. You let them linger because you're timing yourself doing the easy sudoku puzzle and you can't let anything throw you off.

12:18 p.m.: Finish the easy sudoku. Any self-respecting sudoku player takes less than three minutes to complete the easy version. You start on the medium and hard versions, and if you finish them all you call it the trifecta.

12:30 p.m.: Lunch arrives.

12:45 p.m.: While eating, look over and see the monologue jokes still sitting on your desk. Take them into Conan's office and hand them to him right away. It's late, he says. Blame the writers.

1:00 p.m.: Conan gets called down to rehearsal.

1:05 p.m.: It's time to socialize. You visit cubicles and catch up with friends. Talk about what everyone had for lunch. Compare notes.

2:00 p.m.: Get back to your desk and answer some emails finally.

2:30 p.m.: Get bored and go to the kitchen for a snack. Stand in front of the snacks for a while trying to figure out what to eat.

2:50 p.m.: Take a much-deserved walk outside to unwind.

3:15 p.m.: Run into your friend who works on a show in a nearby soundstage. Go for a fun ride in the golf cart and catch up.

3:30 p.m.: Go to Conan's dressing room for a preshow meeting with Andy, Jeff Ross, and the writers.

4:30 p.m.: Showtime. Watch from the green room or from your desk while doing the crossword puzzle.

5:00 p.m.: Show ends.

5:30 p.m.: After the postshow meeting, Conan comes back upstairs and asks if there are any messages. You say no, but you see the red light blinking on your phone. You hope he doesn't see it. You realize you didn't get any actual work done all day. You do your best to convince him it was just a normal day with nothing exciting going on and hope you're right. He goes into his office. You check your emails to make sure there weren't any big issues or emergencies or important messages. Most of the time there aren't. You did it. You managed to get nothing of any substance done, and you got away with it because you clearly have no morals. You have managed to make everyone around you lower their standards to such a point that they can send you an email and not get a response for several hours and no one makes a peep about it. You also ate way too much food, and you tell yourself starting tomorrow you'll stop snacking so much and maybe even start bringing in your own food. Realize you won't do that and hate yourself for your lack of willpower.

6:00 p.m.: Go home.

THE AVERAGE WORK DAY

Danny + Jennifer Aniston

No one has prepared me for my job better than my brother, Danny. I had a twenty-six-year training period to ready myself for the teasing, getting made fun of, and everything else a brother might do to torture his younger sister.

If I was lying down on the couch, he would take a pillow, put it on my head, and sit on it until my pleas for him to get up became more petrified. When we were in high school, Danny was a defensive lineman for our high school's football team. If I was standing around the house, not paying attention, he would get into his football stance and charge at me and tackle. Actually tackle me. I like to think I contributed to the team's undefeated season in some small way. When we were in the car and I would plead for Danny to stop touching my arm, he would hold his hand an inch away and say "I'm not touching you" to the point of unbelievable irritation. After we watched *The Shawshank Redemption*, he called me Alexander as a code for calling me a dumbass because one of the characters in the movie incorrectly pronounced Alexandre Dumas's last name as "dumbass." It was Danny's code for calling me something he knew our parents wouldn't approve of. If I ever pleaded to my parents to discipline him, they would smile and say, "That's how he shows you he loves you." Enablers.

Conan and I have a similar dynamic. He is more of an archnemesis than a boss. It's important to both of us that we get the last word in a conversation. On the podcast, there have been moments when we've been having a discussion and our idiotic need to get the last word has bled into the recording. For a time, we would obsessively play tag. There were moments when, before the show, Conan would lock himself in the bathroom so I couldn't get to him. We had a five-minute rule—if I couldn't get to him after five minutes, then he would win. The sheer idiocy. The amount of time wasted. The frustration I felt and feel even recounting what we would do. Saying "I touched you last!" to a talk show legend right before he would run through his monologue so he wouldn't have time to chase after me and punch my arm was the absolute definition of stupid. But the times I won made me stronger, much like the times I would get the better of Danny.

My brother and I couldn't be more different. I had an eclectic group of friends in high school—a circle comprising the photo editor for the paper, drama students, a former cheerleader, and other random young men and women who weren't popular but weren't socially shunned either. A friend of mine has a theory that either people hated high school, or it was the best time of their lives. I told her that for my friends and me, high school was just somewhere in the middle—those four years were fun, awkward, and not at all an era that defined us. I was a very mediocre student. I scored a 1080 on the SATs and I remember seeing the average at the time was 1000. I took it a second time and had the exact same score. I got some As, mostly Bs, and some Cs. It wasn't until I got to college that I really applied myself and became obsessive about my grades. I was determined to show that while my transcript was average, I was capable of so much more. While I started off as a mediocre student in high school, I became studious and took on extracurricular activities that would give me a résumé that could set me apart.

Danny was totally different. When he went to college, he joined a fraternity and didn't stress about his grades like I did. He had known exactly what he wanted to do since he was very young, which is odd because he wanted to work in finance. There's a photo of my family from when I was a child—my mom, dad, grandmother, grandfather, great-grandmother, Danny, and me all in our living room on what looks to be an uneventful day. We're all dressed casually except for my brother, who is wearing a suit, standing prominently in the photo with a stoic face. He couldn't have been more than ten years old.

Having a job in finance had been his dream since youth, so that's what he worked for. Thanks to his focus to get there, he had a job waiting for him when he graduated college and has thrived ever since. I was always the kooky sibling. The one who wanted to work in TV and got a part-time job after I graduated from a private university that had put me in debt. Our differences are what drive our biggest disagreements, but they're also some of the things I love about my brother. Now as adults, our differences make our friendship stronger.

It was an enormous treat for me to invite my brother to watch a taping when Jennifer Aniston was on the show.

As kids, we would watch *Friends* as a family. That was

when Danny developed a crush on Jennifer Aniston, a woman he has described as "perfect" countless times. She was his ideal and continued to be his idea of perfection long after the show went off the air. Everyone knows it, including Danny's wife, Lucy. So when Jennifer Aniston was booked on the show, the first person I texted was Danny, who jumped at the idea of coming to the taping. I loved that I had a chance to show my brother what I did for a living and give him an opportunity to see his "perfect woman" in person.

When I get people tickets to a taping, I can either get them a pass to go through a VIP line or arrange it so they can come through the green room, which is an option I reserve only for my family and closest friends. Danny and Lucy both left work early and came to the taping together, and I met them in the green room. They were escorted to their seats, then came back to the green room after the show to say bye and leave. That was when the worst thing that has ever happened to me occurred.

Jennifer Aniston had stayed throughout the duration of the show and was leaving while Danny, Lucy, and I were in the green room. The three of us were leaning on a credenza facing the wall where her dressing room was, catching up and talking about the show. Jennifer Aniston emerged from her room in all her ethereal beauty, flanked by her reps, and floated toward us to walk out the green room door. As she was walking, she looked up, then glanced back down and did a double take. She smiled at someone next to me, dare I say flirtatiously. She took a finger and playfully brushed one of her healthy, legendary locks away from her face. Then, with a quick turn, she was gone.

I had witnessed a double-take, flirty-smile hair flip. And it came from Jennifer Aniston. What made me think she was flirting? For starters, a flirt knows a flirt. I've given that look to guys in bars, and the last time I gave that look to someone, I ended up marrying him. There was something about the smile and the way she played with her hair that made me think someone in the green room was a very lucky man.

I immediately looked in the direction she had smiled, and I saw my dumb brother, with a giant grin plastered on his face. It was him. He was the one. The recipient of the hair flick. I wanted to barf.

He looked at us and said, "Did you see that?"

I quickly looked over at Lucy, hoping she had missed it. If I was the only one who had seen it, I could lie and say it meant nothing or that I had been looking elsewhere. Lucy was also hoping I hadn't seen it, but when we both realized we had seen the same thing (we *think*), then we knew we couldn't pretend. And boy, were we right to be filled with dread.

He brings it up at Thanksgiving dinner.

He brings it up when we're having a family beach day.

He brings it up when he and I are catching up on the phone.

Sometimes he'll call me when he's hanging out with his friends because he wants me to corroborate his story. Without Lucy and me witnessing Jennifer Aniston playfully flipping her hair at my brother, he'd just be another guy making shit up about a beautiful woman who he hoped would pay attention to him. But he's not. I was there and I saw it and I hate that I can't deny it.

In my time working for Conan, I have never once had a moment like that. A look might seem so inconsequential, but the possibility is what keeps Danny going. What if his wife and sister hadn't been there cockblocking him? What if he had said something to her and she reciprocated and he became one of her great loves?

But there's also the possibility the look meant nothing. That he would've smiled back, said something to her, and she would've graciously rebuffed his advances and life would carry on. The frustrating thing for me, his sister, is that we'll never know. The possibility of something more is there, lingering in the air. The idea that maybe Jennifer Aniston thought my brother, the same guy who would eat all my food before I even sat down at the dinner table, was handsome. It's offensive to me that one of the most beautiful women in the world would think that my brother, the same guy who would unapologetically use all my hair product without asking, was worth even smiling at. The idea that Jennifer Aniston, an actress on arguably the most popular sitcom ever, would think that my brother, the same guy who would throw his socks at me after his football practice, would have any interest in my brother after she was married to Brad Pitt. BRAD. PITT. No, ma'am. The narrative I'm going with is that it meant nothing, and she was merely being nice, but the problem is that I don't know *for sure* and that small chance that she was actually interested in him is what fuels him.

It's a moment that will haunt me forever. When we're eighty, Danny will be there telling his grandkids about the time one of the most beautiful actresses *of all time* flirtatiously smiled at him when he went to a TV taping. Then, after explaining what TV was, he'll look at me and say, "Your great-aunt Sona can vouch for me." And there I'll be, wishing I'd had him go through the VIP line.

Last-Minute Guest on the Show

Silicon Valley used to be one of my favorite shows on TV. That is, until their production schedule forced Kumail Nanjiani to cancel his appearance on our show at the last minute. After that, I never watched another episode. Why? Because thanks to Kumail's last-minute cancellation, I had to fill in as the guest for that night's show.

Throughout the day, we had heard rumblings that there was a possibility Kumail was going to be unable to make the taping in time, but it wasn't until thirty minutes before showtime that the team got the official word that he had to cancel. I was in Conan's dressing room at the time with Jeff Ross, Matt O'Brien, and Mike Sweeney as they brainstormed how to fill the time. Conan was eerily calm, which is never a good sign. I was asked to leave the room to give them some privacy, which I thought was especially weird. Why would they need privacy to discuss the content? I had a bad feeling.

I killed some time sitting on the couch in the green room, eating cheese, as I do. There was a lovely aged gouda we would get from catering and the Boursin cheese I love. With the right crackers, it made my mouth so happy, and at times, I found myself to be the only one indulging in the cheese plate. It's an embarrassing thing to be lost in a cheese trance and not realize you are the only one going to town on a plate meant for twenty people. I skipped the proper etiquette of taking a reasonable amount of cheese and crackers and placing it on a small personal plate and went straight for the entrée-size platter as if the spread of cheese, crackers, fruits, and spreads had been put together for me and no one else. I didn't forget the manners I learned in Girl Scouts, though—I would use the small plastic tongs catering provided to delicately pull a cracker from the pile, then grab a small plastic knife to pile an unhealthy amount of cheese onto said cracker, then indelicately shove the entire thing into my overly eager mouth. Normally I would worry about the guest for the night seeing me in my cheese frenzy, but we didn't even have a guest for that night, so who could care?

As I was stuffing my face, Jeff walked out of Conan's dressing room and told me to go to makeup. That was it—he didn't offer an explanation as to why or what was happening, so I just did as I was told. By this point, I was actively ignoring the obvious. Or maybe the cheese had slowed my senses. Either way, I loved getting my makeup done by the artists in the dressing room, so happily I went. You think you know how to put on eye shadow until a professional does it for you; then you realize you're just a monster with a brush.

I'm sitting in the chair getting my makeup done, and one

of our supervising producers, JP Buck, walks in and starts asking me questions, like he's doing a pre-interview. JP finally told me what I already feared, that I would be filling in for Kumail as the guest on that night's show. Thank God I had washed my hair that day.

I had nothing interesting to say. I'm not famous. I didn't have funny material prepared. I was wearing jeans and a white shirt, so I didn't have any sexy clothes to distract people with. I didn't know what I was supposed to talk about with Conan, and I had no idea what I was supposed to do. Erin Gillman, our talent coordinator, wrote my name on a Post-it note and stuck it on one of the dressing rooms. I sat there, watching the top of the show, hoping Conan would kill enough time with the audience that they wouldn't need me after all. No one worked the room like Conan, and I thought if he just got on a roll, maybe my problem would be solved. I even thought about how wonderful it would be if he took someone out of the audience and made them do the guest spot on the show. So riveting! I would watch that!

You can imagine my absolute horror when someone came in to put the goddamn microphone on me. This was really happening.

I know there are people who dream of this moment their entire lives. I can't think of anything more exciting for an up-and-comer than to be sitting in the seat between Conan O'Brien and Andy Richter. But I'm not an up-and-comer. I like to eat cheese in the dressing room while watching other people's dreams play out.

It's not that I wasn't excited. It's that I really didn't think I was going to contribute anything. I sit next to Andy every day in the preshow meeting. I would take that over sitting next to him on the show any day. We make inappropriate jokes and laugh and disrupt the meeting, and it's fun. Now I had to make sure I didn't slip up and say anything that would shame my whole family.

When I first got out there, I was nervous, but as soon as the first laugh came, I just calmed down. I figured I had nothing to lose. If I was terrible, who cares. I was going to get offstage and just go back upstairs to my desk anyway. If everything went great, that was fine, too. I would still go back upstairs to my desk after. Nothing in my life would change either way, and I kept telling myself that. If I put too much importance on that moment, I would've never liked the way the interview went. I just kept telling myself, "It's not like you're in the finals at speech nationals." *That* was a scary moment, the culmination of years of hard work, something I really cared about. This was not that.

I'm sure if I had been booked earlier, I would have obsessively worried about every aspect of my appearance: What was I wearing? What color should I paint my nails? How should I wear my hair? Should I dress casual or wear something a little more formal? Being a last-minute fill-in removed any of those worries for me—I was able to focus on just having a good time being out onstage with two people I trusted. I couldn't stress because I didn't have time to stress. There were also zero stakes and no expectations. A while after my appearance, I did a quick interview with *Variety* for a piece on Conan and podcasting, and they asked me about my appearance as a guest on Conan's show. This was the quote from the piece:

> *"It shouldn't happen again," she says. "I did well because the expectations were very low. When you put a random assistant on camera and they don't throw up on themselves, you think they did a good job."*

It was over quickly. I asked someone in the audience who had been referenced by Conan earlier in the monologue if he had any weed on him. I talked about the time I texted Conan about my dog throwing up and he thought I was talking about myself. (My dog's name is Oki. I texted Conan, "Oki threw up and shit everywhere," and he misread the text and thought I had typed out "Okay, I threw up and shit everywhere.") By the end of the segment, I had the audience chanting "buy her a house" after I took the opportunity to ask Conan if he'd buy me and my husband a house. I enjoyed it much more than I thought I would. I went back to the green room, and my coworkers who watch the show from there all applauded when I walked in, which felt great. I had champagne and more cheese. I called to let my family know I would be on the show so they would watch. Then I just walked back upstairs to my desk. I didn't know how people would perceive it or if anyone would care, but I knew that I felt okay about it, even though I had known it was never going to be as big a moment for me as speech nationals.

My Car

My car has always been so important to me. I've never had an expensive or extravagant car—just one that's reliably taken me from point A to point B. I was always a VW Jetta girl from the moment I got my license to the moment I realized they're not actually great cars.

Like a lot of young Angelenos, I got my license the second I turned sixteen. I took my license picture right after I took the SATs, and the awful photo on my license haunted me for many years after. I would present my ID to bouncers at a bar and they would actually cringe at the sight of my license photo: a slight smile big enough to barely show the braces I had for way too long, my hair up in a messy bun with a rogue curl sticking out, an ill-fitting T-shirt accentuated by an ill-fitting hoodie. It was all a mess, but I digress.

It was 1998, and the first car I drove around was my dad's '92 VW Jetta. My father was the general manager for a lunch truck catering warehouse, and whenever something was wrong with his car, he'd have the mechanics at the warehouse fix it. If the car had trouble starting with the turn of the key, you simply had to push a button affixed to the left of the wheel that would turn the car on. It was odd, and my friends who drove in the car thought it was odd. There was also a bat in the trunk that you would use to hit a specific spot in the engine in case you were still having trouble turning the car on. And there was always a spare bottle of antifreeze. My dad took great care of his car, but it was just old. The odometer showed 300,000 miles, and that was before the odometer stopped working. FM radio didn't work, so we had to exclusively listen to AM radio when we were in the car. That is how I got acquainted with Radio Disney. When I got my license, I drove the car more than my father did, ostensibly ruining it. After I started driving it, it lasted only two more years and then spontaneously combusted in the driveway. When I say "spontaneously combusted," I mean that in a literal sense. The car was sitting in the driveway and, apropos of nothing, the engine caught fire. We put it out before it could get worse, but that was the end of the '92 Jetta.

Shortly after that, my parents surprised me with a used '97 Jetta that I loved. My dad had to remind me to make sure I got basic maintenance done on the car, like oil changes and tune-ups. This car also eventually had its quirks. I had put a CD in the CD player once, and it never came out. Some doors would unlock and others wouldn't, but the doors that would work or not work always changed. Sometimes the sunroof would get stuck open and I would pray it wouldn't rain that day. Luckily we were in LA, so it wasn't an issue, although there was the constant threat of theft.

That car kept me on my toes. I had to get the transmission on that car replaced . . . twice. One day, about seven years after I first got the car, I was driving to work from my parents' house and the car made a noise as though there was something metal dragging underneath it. I went back to my parents' house and borrowed my mom's car for the day and gave her the keys to my car. She took my car to her yoga class, which was nearby. On her way back, the car was climbing up a steep hill, and suddenly my mom felt what she thought was a flat tire. When she got out of the car, she saw both the tire and the rim bouncing down the hill. She stood there in her yoga clothes with her yoga mat, trying to get some help. Someone saw her, and instead of stopping, they called the police. When the police came, my mom explained what had happened and they offered to drive her back home. Because she was a civilian, she had to ride in the backseat, where criminals sit. In her yoga clothes.

My dad was pretty upset when he found out I had barely done any of the basic upkeep he constantly implored me to do. Apparently it was my fault that I had driven this car into the ground. When I went back to their house to drop my mom's car off, it was decided that I should get a new car, which was devastating. Throughout all my time driving that Jetta, I had formed quite the attachment to it—it was the car I had driven to college, to my first apartment, to countless dates, and to so much more. I was actually sobbing when we traded it in for my 2007 Jetta.

Unlike the other two cars I had driven, this one was brand-new. And I had paid for all of it. I drove it for years and developed a true feeling of love toward it. It was such a point of pride for me to own a car, but this, too, had its issues. And that's where Conan comes in.

There was always something new that was wrong with my car—the light would never turn off, the sunglass holder would never close, the electrical was always off. The fabric on the roof of the car was drooping down considerably. I constantly had to take it to the shop to get it fixed. It was a huge pain in the ass.

In 2018, Conan and the writers thought it would be fun if he and I went online car shopping together. With a partnership with Autotrader, we shot a remote where he essentially shat on my car for about six minutes, and then we went online to look at whatever cars were available.

While Conan was making fun of my car, he ripped off the sunglass holder, took out the bulb from the light fixture, and stuffed magazines into the fabric hanging down from my roof. All this in front of rolling cameras. Our field producer, Jason Chillemi, came after we were done shooting to "fix" whatever Conan had done to my car, but he couldn't fix it. I always thought our team fixed anything Conan broke, especially if it was personal property. But as I sat there clutching my sunglass holder, realizing it would not be fixed, I came to terms with the fact that my bulb would not be replaced and that even more damage to the hanging fabric in my backseat would now be more permanent. My car started off as a piece of shit, and after we shot the segment for the show, it was an even bigger piece of shit.

Two months after we shot the remote, I was driving in heavy LA traffic on the 134 freeway from Burbank to Glendale. I remember I had stopped because of gridlock, and when I put my foot on the gas to accelerate, nothing happened. Panic began to set in, and I put my car in neutral and rolled to the shoulder. People are not nice about rolling cars on the freeway. I called my husband crying and told him what had happened—that my piece-of-shit Jetta would not accelerate and it had no power. He came to get me, and we had the car towed to a nearby mechanic, who charged me $500 to fix what he thought was the problem (I should've been skeptical of this mechanic when he only looked at my husband to explain what was going on with the car and completely ignored my presence . . . like I didn't pay for the fucking thing). A day after we got my car back from the shop, the exact same thing happened to me in the exact same spot on the freeway. This time, I just towed it home, cleared out my things, said my goodbyes, and towed it to the nearest CarMax, where I got $700 for it.

The segment with my car prompted fans who we interacted with to ask if Conan ever bought me a new car, as if he's Oprah. So he did it, but in the most passive-aggressive Conan way possible. The car Conan bought me was the one he presented to me on the air—a disgusting Honda that looked like someone had been murdered in it that he bought for about $500, which, in my opinion, was $400 too much. To me, that segment is much more than a reminder of how terrible I am at upkeeping a car—it's a reminder of the milestones I hit while owning the cars I drove. When I first bought my '07 Jetta, I was a coordinator at NBC. When I finally got rid of it, I was taking pictures with it to update the hordes of Conan fans.

I now drive a Kia Niro, a sensible and reliable hybrid. When my lease ends, I'll be trading it in for a minivan because I'm now a mother of two. If I'm ever feeling nostalgic, I'll look back at that comedy segment we did and remember not just that Jetta but all the Jettas that came before it, a reminder of my life's mobility in this city.

The Podcast

In 2018, Conan called me into his office to have a quick chat. He told me he was launching a podcast and he wanted me to be on it with him as a regular. I am hard-pressed to call myself his cohost because he does all the heavy lifting, and I just chill on the sidelines, jumping in whenever it makes the most sense. I probably shouldn't have revealed how easy I think my contributions to the podcast are because it takes away my leverage when I want a raise, but it's safe to say I went from being the World's Worst Assistant to the World's Worst . . . Sidekick? I don't know. All I know is I was worried initially about being on the podcast because I'm not a comedy professional.

I never thought I would be a contributor in any way to content when I first signed on to be Conan's assistant. I legitimately believed I would work for him for five years at the most, then move on to the next thing, but twelve years later, I'm still around. Conan asking me to be a part of his podcast was equal parts exciting and terrifying. But here's the thing—I'm a speech champion.

I know I've brought this up before in this book, and if I brought it up only once or twice, it's still less than the number of times I bring it up on a weekly basis in my regular life. When was I a national speech champion, you might be wondering? In the spring of 2003. *But, Sona, isn't that almost twenty years ago?* Why yes. Yes, it is. *Isn't that too long to be holding on to an accomplishment?* Yes, that is also true.

I think this is as good a time as any to talk about it some more. At this point, everyone who knows me or has met me for even ten minutes is rolling their eyes. I can only imagine my brother's or even Conan's annoyance at having to read about my national speech championship after years of hearing about the time I won a national speech championship. So why bring it up now?

It's not because some of the friends I made in speech are still some of my closest friends in life. It's not because I'm calm when talking in a public setting. And it's not because I have a slew of trophies, and trophies make me feel good. It's because that's where I learned self-confidence.

I'll back up.

After high school, I went to a community college in Walnut, California, called Mt. San Antonio College. I had graduated from a high school somewhat nearby, and a few of my other friends also enrolled there. I liked that it was almost an extension of my high school years. My plan when I first got to college was to make every semester different. In the fall semester of my freshman year, I tried out for the college production of *One Flew Over the Cuckoo's Nest* and was cast as Sandy, a random prostitute who comes to party at the institution. None of this is relevant, only to say this is the extent of my acting résumé.

That same semester I took a speech class with a professor named Liesel Reinhart. One day early on in the semester, Liesel gave us an assignment to put together a presentation for a new ride at an amusement park based on a movie. Liesel wanted to give an example to the class and asked for a movie that no one would ever make an amusement park ride out of, and I yelled out without hesitation, "*The Bridges of Madison County*!" Yes, it *is* sad that I remember a joke no one except Liesel really laughed at. Anyway, Liesel wasn't much older than I was, and she became a great friend and mentor. She's actually the one who told me to write this book. She's also the one who told me to join the speech team. Still, none of this is relevant, and I'm sorry. I'm getting to the point, albeit very slowly.

It wasn't until my second semester during my second year at a two-year college that I decided to take another speech-related course called Readers Theater, taught by Liesel's boyfriend, Steve. It was in this class that I found out the other term for speech and debate competition in college is "forensics." I found out because Steve had to tell people who were hoping to get into a CSI-type job that they were in the wrong class on the first day. A few people walked out. Anyway, according to the website for the American Readers Theater Association, Readers Theater is "a style of group performance combining aspects of traditional theater with aspects of public address, performance art, oral interpretation, dance, and more." We did an entire Readers Theater on the concept of building things called "Build," and in one part, we all had to sing a melody. After we practiced it one time, Steve said, "That sounded okay.

Let's try it without Sona," and that's when I found out I have a horrible singing voice. Anyway, again, NOT RELEVANT. The class, however, gave me the opportunity for my first foray into speech competition.

The following year (and if you're following, this is the THIRD year of my time at a two-year college), I joined the speech team full-on. I had always seen the signs they posted on campus saying "Don't You Want to Be a National Champion in Something?" and I thought, "Well, I'm not going to be a champion, but maybe I'll get close."

I hit the ground running.

Forensics is split into two types of speech: interpretive and platform. Interpretive speeches are ones that involve more performance (speeches based on plays or prose or poems that present an idea or concept). Platform speeches are ones that you write and include informative and persuasive speeches. And like a champion, I did it all.

I was in a duo (an interpretive speech with two people performing) based on a play called *The Baddest Natashas*, by Juliana Francis-Kelly, where two Victorian-era prostitutes are juxtaposed with a modern-era actress auditioning for roles. It was insane.

I wrote about my culture in a speech called "ArmeniaMania." It was a speech to entertain (or an after-dinner speech), which is supposed to be funny.

I did a speech on "warchalking," a system whereby people mark on buildings that have open Wi-Fi signals—i.e., Wi-Fi networks without password protection.

I did a dramatic speech based on a one-woman show by Lisa Kron called *2.5 Minute Ride and 101 Humiliating Stories*.

I did another duo with a friend based on a short play called *Quake*, by Melanie Marnich, about a woman who is looking for the love of her life.

I also dipped my toes into extemporaneous speaking. You spend all year putting together a big file of articles about world events from trusted sources; then, when the round starts, you get a series of questions and prepare a ten-minute sourced speech responding to one of the questions. It's very difficult.

When I first saw that sign on campus talking about being a national champion in something, I never thought I could get that far, but I knew it would be worth aspiring to get close. By the end of the year, after many competitions, I wouldn't settle for anything less. I remember one of my coaches talking about winning a round before you even start speaking. Your confidence alone can win the round for you. For a long time while I was competing, I didn't fully understand that. It wasn't until three different episodes with my coaches that I finally got what they meant.

The first time was an episode during a tournament in Pasadena. I had made it to the finals for the after-dinner speech event with two other people, who were coincidentally on my team as well. The finals for this particular event were in front of every participant in the entire competition—about four hundred people. The first finalist went up and delivered his speech flawlessly. Then the second competitor, again, flawless. Then it was my turn. I went up there and started my speech perfectly.

About a third into it, I just . . . blanked. There was nothing. I began to panic. Four hundred sets of eyes were looking at me, and I was saying nothing. I looked straight into the eyes of someone in the first row and gave them a look that conveyed "Can you please tell me what my speech is supposed to say here?" But how would they know? No one would know. I was alone. After a silence that felt like it was twenty minutes long but was probably more like twenty seconds, I stared at the ground and clapped once. The clap echoed through this full yet completely silent room. I felt people in the front row looking at me with pity, thrilled they weren't in my shoes. I wanted to stop doing the speech right there and just sit on the floor and curl up into the fetal position and suck on my thumb like a baby.

But I didn't. I eventually remembered my speech, then delivered the rest of it flawlessly. When I sat down at my seat, my teammates were quick to console me. Some of them didn't even realize I had forgotten my speech until I reminded them I clapped once in the beginning as a way of trying to remember my stupid speech. The clap became known on my team as "The Clap Heard 'Round the World."

When it came time to announce first, second, and third place, I had zero hope. I braced myself for the third-place finish, only I didn't come in third. I tied for second. Even with my monthlong pause, I tied my teammate for second place. One of the judges came up to me afterward and said that if I hadn't briefly forgotten my speech, I would've won. That was the first big boost of confidence I got during competitions.

The second time, we were at an overnight competition

somewhere near San Diego. We all got hotel rooms and would practice our speeches ad nauseam to make sure they were perfect for the next day's competition. This particular night, I was practicing my speech with Liesel and Adam, another member of the team and a dear friend. I kept doing my piece over and over again, and Liesel kept telling me something was missing from it, then asked me why I wasn't putting any confidence into my piece. She kept saying that I was saying all the words right and that my performance was fine, but that I was lacking the kind of conviction that only comes with self-confidence. I didn't fully understand how my self-confidence could work itself into my piece. Our practice became a therapy session of sorts, and I started crying. I *thought* I was a confident person, though looking back now, I realize I wasn't. I always had issues with ambition, as if I was comfortable in the middle, the 50th percentile. I didn't allow myself to think I deserved more than that, as though striving for more and deserving more weren't meant for me. That night in the hotel room, I was a wreck. I took everything that was said to me to heart and really worked on myself. For every tournament we went to after that night, I either won or placed with my speeches.

The third time the coaches led me to a personal reckoning was when we were at nationals in Portland. We went there a few nights before the final so we could all fine-tune our speeches. I had five pieces I took to nationals, and I felt like they were all in good shape. At times, all fourteen students who were competing and the four coaches who were with us would convene in a room, and we would perform our speeches for the team. One day, I went up there thinking I was about to nail my performance, but when I started, the coaches stopped me a few lines in and told me to restart. Then they did that again. Then again.

"Wait, start again. I don't feel like you're really feeling it in that part."

"Stop, you're fumbling too many words. Start again."

"Stop, you're rushing through it. Start from the beginning."

I lost it. I just stopped in the middle of my performance and went to the bathroom and started crying. I'm a crier. I remember getting so frustrated, and I didn't know what else to do. I was strutting around like I was crushing it, but my cockiness was making me complacent. It didn't seem to matter if I was starting my speech correctly; the coaches' intention was to break me down. And break me down they did. They were taking me out of my comfort zone and stripping me down in front of the entire team. When I lost it, I was able to compose myself and get back into the room stronger because of it. I'll never forget how I felt in that moment. And it worked. Out of my five events, I got gold in three of them and bronze in a fourth. I was one point away from breaking into semifinals in extemporaneous speaking. That point haunts me to this day.

So I started out thinking a trophy would be nice, but by the end of our season, I didn't want just one trophy; I wanted them all. More importantly, I felt as though I had worked hard enough to *deserve* them.

Wow, okay, I don't know what this tangent was all about. I started talking about the podcast and somehow that bled into talking about being a national speech champion. Here we go, back on track. So many people ask me if I was nervous (or am nervous) about being on a podcast with Matt Gourley, who is a podcasting legend and a brilliant improv mind, and Conan, who is a massive figure in comedy. My honest answer is always no. I'm not trying to go head-to-head with them with comedy, and it's hard to fail when you peaked in 2003. That's right, the reason I just spent so long explaining my speech-competition journey to you is because that is when I peaked. I wasn't going to write an entire book and not find a way to tell that whole story from start to finish. Obviously.

You know how there's always that one girl in high school who you can't stand because you guys went to elementary school together and she yelled out that you needed a bra when she was at the peak of her swing, high enough for everyone at recess to hear, and you went to a different junior high, so you didn't see her again until high school, and when you did, there she was, still very beautiful and skinny and dating that one guy everyone was in love with, but then you saw her on Facebook like twelve years later and she's aged poorly and she's clearly miserable and you realize she peaked in high school? Well, speech was when I peaked. I'm not embarrassed by it. I'm *empowered* by it. When you peaked and you know you did, everything that follows has zero pressure.

What's that? I'm going to take my first-ever trip to Armenia and there will be a film crew with me and it will be televised? Cool, let's do this.

What's that? We're going to Washington, DC, for a taping of *Christmas in Washington* and the Obamas will all be there? Bring it on.

What's that? I'm going to the Emmys to cheer on our team for *The Tonight Show with Conan O'Brien*? Sounds like fun!

So when Conan asked me if I would be interested in doing the podcast with him, I emphatically said yes. Of course I would. And I wasn't nervous because (a) I'm clearly comfortable with public speaking and (b) I peaked a long time ago. Knowing I don't have anything to lose allows me to just be myself and to really enjoy everything I get to experience with the podcast, yes, but also in my strange and amazing life as Conan's assistant. I can comfortably sit across from Lin-Manuel Miranda describing the nuances behind the masterpiece that is "Under Pressure" without feeling like I have to make a joke. I can sit across from Michelle Obama in a classroom in Milwaukee as Conan interviews her without worrying about how I come across. I can sit in a Zoom interview with Shaquille O'Neal and listen as he comes up with names for my twins without losing my shit. (The names he came up with at first were Mark and Markus. When we said they were too similar, he changed his suggestion to Mark and Marco.) Why don't I worry when we're recording? Because I've felt pressure before, and pressure is reciting a ten-minute memorized speech on very little sleep while wearing a suit and heels in a hotel room in Portland. That's pressure.

The major change that did occur after the podcast,

however, was the feeling that I had officially gone from being an assistant to being "talent." My name is on merch, a cashier at Trader Joe's recognized me just because of my voice, and I've been a part of a live recording of our podcast in front of thousands of people. The best thing about the podcast is that it came naturally, as if someone put a microphone in front of Conan and me and we were just having our normal repartee. Hearing people say they like it is the biggest testament to how my relationship with Conan has evolved. Back when I first started working for Conan, I would've never had the comfort level with him that I have now, but after more than a decade I'm able to speak with him candidly because I feel security in our friendship.

Even considering all that, the best part about the podcast has been meeting Matt Gourley. Matt grew up in Whittier, which is about fifteen minutes away from where I grew up in Hacienda Heights. We're two SoCal kids, and getting to know him has been a pure delight. Listening to him riff with Conan is among my favorite things when we record.

With the podcast, I can show up and be me. And after all the work I've done on myself over the years, I'm more than happy with that.

Trip to Armenia

In early 2015, President Obama relaxed travel restrictions to Cuba. Within weeks, Conan took a crew there to shoot an international special. It was so well received by both audiences and critics that Conan decided to make international travel specials a new part of his career.

When it came time to discuss what the second special would be, we had meetings to brainstorm and everyone would throw out these incredibly exotic countries . . . all of which would've been fantastic. Conan chimed in at one point and said, "Why don't we take Sona to Armenia?"

My stomach dropped when everyone agreed.

I'm a proud Armenian-American. I was born in Montebello, California, and there's a robust Armenian community there. We have a church and a school and a community center. The Armenians started immigrating to Montebello around the '60s. That's when my dad came, as the community really established itself as a part of that Los Angeles suburb. I was absorbed into that small but mighty group of people from a very early age, and being Armenian became a very important part of my identity.

And now, for my very first trip to the homeland, I was going with the whitest man I know with a crew that consisted of no Armenians, all to be televised nationally. I was sure Conan and everyone wouldn't embarrass me, but there was still this hint of worry in the back of my mind. What if the special was awful? This community that I love and am so proud to be a part of might hate it. They might disown me.

I tried not to think about it.

To be honest, I didn't even fully believe the trip was happening until we were wheels up on our way. Then we landed in Armenia, and I remember getting off the plane and seeing people who looked and sounded like so many people I know. I don't speak the dialect of Armenian they speak in Armenia, so my communication suffered. Armenian is a complicated language, and the dialects are completely different between regions—to the point that it can be difficult understanding and speaking with people who use a different dialect. To make matters worse, I even have trouble speaking the dialect I grew up speaking. It was a linguistic mess.

After our trip to the Garni temple, where Conan danced with traditional Armenian dancers, we went to a house nearby and watched women make lavash, Armenian bread. They also made oghi, which is a liquor that tastes like black licorice. We had a translator with us the whole time who was a major help, but they wanted to shoot the piece where Conan and I spoke to the gentleman who made oghi without a translator so it wouldn't slow down the process. We had to rely on my poor communication skills to translate the process by which oghi is made. Luckily, the man didn't understand English, so I just made everything up. He would gesture to different pipes and parts of the apparatus, and I would just mimic him and make up complete nonsense.

"Something in eastern-dialect Armenian" is what I would hear while he pointed to a giant vat of something.

"This vat holds the alcohol and allows it to really ferment during the process by which the liquor is made and it allows the alcohol to become a drink you can drink" is what I would say while pointing to the same vat.

"More Armenian I don't understand," as he pointed to a pipe

that led to a spigot where the finished product would come out from.

"This pipe is where the alcohol finds its way to this spigot and you can drink the oghi and have a good time with your friends and the alcohol will loosen you up because it's strong, and I don't know why he was emphatic when he was talking about this pipe here" is what I would say as I made the same gestures.

The trick was to speak quickly and say a lot of words just in case he understood basic English. Luckily he would just nod along while I was "translating" what he was saying, as if he was agreeing with my explanation of the process of which he was a master. He had no idea I was making a complete disgrace of his art. Remember this: people don't change. Here I am, filming a national television special with Conan O'Brien, having a meaningful cultural experience in my homeland, and the bullshit is still flying. This is vintage Sona.

When we got back into the van to return to the hotel, I told everyone I had made up the translations. I had done such a convincing job that no one noticed. We ended up cutting that part out, so it didn't matter anyway.

Even though I grew up as an Armenian-American in the US, with my parents instilling a great pride of my culture in me, I couldn't ignore what made me different in Armenia. One day during our downtime, two of our writers and I went to Vernissage, a bazaar where you can buy virtually anything. As we were leaving, we flagged down a taxi and hopped in. While we were driving, our taxi driver saw a friend of his on the side of the road and stopped in the middle of the street to greet him. As they were having their conversation, it became apparent that the taxi driver's friend needed a ride somewhere, and with our taxi driver having a mode of transportation, what better way for him to get where he needed to be than for the taxi driver to give him a ride? So the friend hops into the car, and we all introduce ourselves and have a lovely ride back to the hotel, where the driver drops us off, then casually drives his friend to the next destination. It would be the same as a taxi in New York City suddenly becoming an UberPool.

But why was this weird to me? Was it because it seemed unprofessional? I've done many unprofessional things in my career, so why did I care? Was it because it just seemed odd? Oddity is another defining characteristic of mine, so again, I wasn't sure why it was such a big deal. It was a moment that stuck out to me, and even now I'm realizing it's not necessarily something I thought was bad, but something I actually respected—going outside the norm of what your job entails and having a good time doing it. I don't even know if he understood what he was doing was abnormal in the eyes of his passengers, but the fact that he didn't care whether we found the whole experience odd was something I . . . admired?

The last night of our trip happened to fall on my birthday. We went to a restaurant called Dolmama and had the entire downstairs area to ourselves. Our waiter made everyone take multiple shots of cognac, which he would light on fire beforehand. I drank a little too much and started hitting on the waiter, who could not have cared less about me. Everyone ate a lot and drank a lot, and at the end of the trip, I had a week's worth of memories that I didn't yet realize would change my life forever.

When we got back from Armenia, our very talented editors sat down with our very talented writers and churned out a special I was more than happy to show to everyone I loved. We had a screening where I invited twenty of my family members, and they all were so happy and proud of the episode.

To this day, the Armenia episode of the Conan Without Borders series is one of my proudest moments in my time working for Conan. But how does it pertain to my being the World's Worst Assistant? Well, it emboldened me. Vulture ranked "Conan in Armenia" as the best of all of Conan's international specials. Conan is an Armenian icon now, and if you live in Montebello, Los Angeles, it really can't get any bigger than that.

The Armenia special is a small piece to a puzzle that, when put together, makes me feel like I'm invincible. I can talk back because the segment we shot with the Armenian matchmaker has over seven million views on YouTube. I feel less remorse about forgetting something because the segment where we buy a rug has almost seven million views. Conan beat his Irish compatriot President Joe Biden in acknowledging the Armenian Genocide by five years, making him a trailblazer with respect to acknowledging crimes against humanity in world history.

HOW TO LEVERAGE YOUR PREGNANCY AT WORK

1: Get a boss who is one of six children and loves his mom.

2: Get pregnant.

PREGNANCY (cont.)

3: Announce your pregnancy early and loudly.

4: Start taking frequent days off due to "doctor's appointments."

5: Once you are pregnant, any food around the office is fair game.

6: Park your car like a boss.

PREGNANCY (cont.)

7: Convince HR to hire an assistant assistant.

8: Get a nod from your favorite celebrity.

The trip to Armenia not only got me more in touch with my roots, but also put me more in the spotlight. Months after the special aired, I rode on the Armenian float in the Rose Parade. I've spoken at many fundraisers and have connected with Armenians all over the world who have seen the special. Non-Armenians have remarked on how much they learned about my culture through the episode.

I had worried about how the show would come across from the moment it was proposed. How could any of the writers, editors, researchers, or even Conan care as much as I did about the way this episode would turn out? They're not Armenian. Something I realized shortly after watching the entire episode, however, is that anyone can make something beautiful about a culture if they're coming at it from a truly curious perspective. Not only did the men and women who were involved in making this episode work tirelessly to make sure it was wonderful, because that's their work ethic, but they wanted to make sure their respect for the culture came through. What I'm most proud of when it comes to the Armenia special is that it was made by non-Armenians who prove you can make something about another culture that those who are part of that culture can be proud of.

A month after the Armenia special aired, my beloved yaya (grandmother) passed away. She is featured in the beginning of the episode when Conan is talking to my family about our upcoming trip to Armenia. To have that video footage of her talking to Conan about how she desperately wants me to find a husband is one of the most treasured moments I have from the episode. I have this perfect documentation of what she became obsessed with in her later years.

Ironically, the episode did in fact lead to me meeting my husband. The following year I was walking around the convention floor at Comic-Con with my friend David Yeh. He ran into his friend Katie Stratton, who was walking around with her friend Tak Boroyan. While David and Katie were catching up, Tak and I started talking, and he eventually recognized me from the Armenia episode. We hit it off instantly, but I wasn't sure if he was dating Katie, so I didn't want to cross a line. The next day, after some cyberstalking, I found out that not only was he single, but he also had sent me a friend request on Facebook months prior after watching the Armenia episode. All I did was accept his friend request, and then, two years later, we were married in a massive Armenian wedding with 550 of our closest friends and family. Yaya would've been so proud.

Covid

During the eleventh season of *Conan*, a global pandemic hit. We left for hiatus in March and never returned. I've noticed Conan always seems to come up with some of his best comedy under extreme pressure, almost as if he welcomes the unexpected. The pandemic was one of those things. We work on the Warner Bros. lot, and they were quick to shut the lot down as soon as the numbers of those afflicted with the Covid-19 virus began to climb.

Conan realized that as long as he continued to make original programming for Turner, the entire staff could continue to get paid without interruption, so he brainstormed. Our writers all started coming up with ideas that could easily be executed via Zoom or that they could shoot in the safety of their own homes, and our bookers began to find guests who could be interviewed virtually. During this time, I became a de facto IT specialist. A small group of us would go to Conan's house regularly to help him out with the technical aspects of shooting the show. We downloaded a prompter app for his laptop and bought tripods, ring lights, and a better camera for his laptop. It was a college-level production, but it worked because everyone's expectations were so low during those early days of the pandemic. There were days when I was the only one they wanted to be at his house in order to better protect him from getting Covid, so of course I had to be extra careful about who I saw and where I went. If Conan got Covid and it was my fault, production could get shut down and it would be on my shoulders. After everything the team had done to make sure we stayed on air, I not only would have felt guilty, but I shudder at the thought of the bits Conan would have come up with at my expense.

We put a system in place. I would go to his house alone to help him out with all the technical aspects of the show. But that didn't last long, and we started bringing a very scaled-down crew to his house to help him shoot. After a few weeks of shooting at his house, we began going to the Largo theater in West Hollywood with a skeleton crew and shooting the show from there. Our field producer Jason Chillemi would have to check our temperatures and oxygen levels every day. We would have to get tested twice a week. It became our new normal, but throughout the course of shooting the show from the Largo, no one got Covid. It was anything but glamorous, but this experience was a bright spot for me during a time when there were very few highlights. It was somewhere for me to go and something for me to do when the only other option was to stay home.

The Largo theater isn't as fancy as our Warner Bros. digs. There are two small dressing rooms backstage, a tiny bathroom, and a small area for snacks. That's the extent of it, but it's incredibly charming, not to mention beloved by the comedy community. The owner, Mark Flanagan (or Flanny, as he's known to everyone), became a dear friend of mine during the months we filmed there. I'd get there at 11 a.m., walk with Flanny to get breakfast and a coffee order for the crew from a lovely coffee shop across the street run by kind New Zealanders, then sit at a small table behind the stage where I'd set up my laptop and work. Even though it was an hourlong commute from my house, I enjoyed the small moments of normalcy that going to work afforded me. That was, of course, until I got pregnant.

My husband and I found out in early November of that year that I was pregnant. When we went to the first ultrasound, we saw two sacs but only one baby, so we figured the other fetus just hadn't developed properly and we celebrated the new addition that would be coming into our lives in July 2021.

The following week, we went for another ultrasound and there were suddenly two babies. Yes, we were having twins. We sat in the room and just stared at each other for a while, allowing the news to soak in. I wasn't just concerned about what a seismic change it would be for our lives, but also about how my body was going to be tested in the months to come. The day after I found out I was pregnant with twins, our IT specialist and good friend Chris Hayes and I went to Conan's house to help him with a virtual fundraiser at his daughter's school. When we got there, Conan asked both of us if we wanted any beer or wine and I said no. Conan immediately asked if I was pregnant. Of course, my boss assumed the only reason I wouldn't want a drink at work must be that I was pregnant. I had to let him know that I was, in fact, pregnant. With twins. He knew before anyone else. From that point on, going to Largo became increasingly difficult. My due date was July 1, 2021, when I'd be having my boys via a scheduled C-section. I got increasingly pregnant, and it became more and more of a liability for me to drive for an hour in the car to get to Largo.

But Conan's show was ending.

During the pandemic, Conan announced he would be leaving *Conan* and would instead be doing a new show for HBO Max. The last show was on June 24, one week before my boys were scheduled to come into the world. I knew I couldn't miss his last shows, so I soldiered on, driving from Altadena to West Hollywood every day. At an appointment with my ob-gyn, I asked him if it was okay for me to continue going to work a month before I was due, and he said, "I really wish you wouldn't." I took his plea as a soft suggestion and continued going. At one point, driving became too difficult, and my husband had to drive me to work. During the last two weeks of shows, it started to become way too uncomfortable for me to sit in a car for an hour, so I was finally forced to slow down. Instead of going every day, I went twice a week. My boys hung in there long enough that I could watch Conan's last network show in person.

David Hopping, Jeff Ross's assistant and my former PA, took over for me while I was on maternity leave. It became clear quickly that he had the eagerness to please that had long since disappeared from my approach to the job. He cared about details I could no longer allow myself to care about, especially now that I was a mother to two babies. When I came back from maternity leave, I told Conan it would be best for David to continue to do the meat of my job, like taking care of Conan's calendar, accompanying him to events and shoots, and being his main point person. David essentially became Conan's assistant, but I was still around as well. I got to the point where I had someone do the bulk of my job while I maintained my position, my grift finally complete. The con was an utter success. I had done it.

During my time working for Conan, my life transformed. I started off as a twenty-six-year-old, ready to take on the television world. I was a happily single party girl, often coming into work hungover. I had a kit with all the essentials (toothbrush, toothpaste, deodorant, etc.) in one of my drawers in case I didn't have time to get myself together before work. By the time I was saying goodbye to the Warner Bros. lot and our show on TBS, I was a thirty-eight-year-old married woman who was pregnant with twins, my kit of essentials barely touched in years. This job saw me through my biggest life transformations, and the more comfortable I got, the more the work suffered. I started off excited to be part of something new, desperate to please. When we said goodbye to the last iteration of Conan's late-night talk show, I had evolved from an eager ingenue to a comfortable adopted member of the O'Brien family. I'm lucky to work for a person who doesn't expect me to sacrifice everything in order to appease him, who lets me be myself and allows me to mess up without making me feel like I'll face dire consequences.

When I first became Conan's assistant, I had no idea what to expect. I had never been someone's personal assistant before, and I had only heard horror stories. I remember asking Tom Supa, Jeff Ross's assistant when I first started working for Conan, what I could do to make sure I didn't mess up at my job, and he told me to err on the side of caution and include all the information I had about anything when inputting things in Conan's calendar or in his contacts. I took that advice to heart and began putting all of myself into this job, and I came out the other end with countless memories and a friend for life. And I did it while being unapologetically myself, warts and all. I didn't set out to be the World's Worst Assistant, but I put in the work, or lack thereof, and discovered my true calling. It's been nothing less than a complete thrill, and I am honored to pass my expertise on to you. Godspeed.

EPILOGUE

IN THE TIME I'VE WORKED FOR CONAN, I'VE HAD THE PLEAsure of some once-in-a-lifetime experiences that have really opened my eyes. More importantly, I've created a friendship with Conan that will go well beyond my time working for him. Conan visited my family after my grandma died, he officiated my best friend's wedding ceremony, he and his wife, Liza, threw my now-husband and me a beautiful engagement party, and he even wrote a letter on our behalf to help us buy our house. Despite the dysfunction, there is an affection there, and I can't imagine being anyone else's terrible assistant.

I will never be the type of person who will compromise their mental and physical well-being for a job. I've gone out of my way to ensure that my happiness in what I'm doing and who I'm working with are my priority, and because of that mentality, I've managed to find a job that I look forward to going to on Mondays. This could never have worked with a different boss—with someone who expected me to sacrifice so much of myself in order to make their life easier. And the sad reality is, there are still so many of those people who expect too much from their subordinates. They pay too little and make unreasonable demands, and what we're left with are people who are cynical and apply that cynicism to what they do after they get promoted (if they ever get promoted).

I realize how lucky I am, but if being the World's Worst Assistant means I get to have a social and personal life as well as a fulfilling career, then I like to think I did something right.

And now, if you'll excuse me, I have to go finish a sudoku puzzle.

ACKNOWLEDGMENTS

My entire life has been filled with overwhelmingly gracious people who've made me feel invincible. Without these people, I never would've felt like I could get away with half the things I've gotten away with.

First, my family. I'm so lucky to have been born into the big, loud, and close Armenian family I was born into. When I first started writing this book, I was a newlywed. When I finished it, I was a mother of newborn twins. My parents, Gulbenk ("Gil") and Nadia, came over every day and watched my babies so I could finish writing this book. But that's only one of the many selfless things they've done for me during my lifetime. I use them as an example every day as I navigate being a new mother.

Even though I dedicated an entire section to him and he's had enough acknowledgment, I have to mention how important my brother has been to me. Danny shaped my sense of humor, and I never would've gotten all I could out of my job if it weren't for him. Plus, he gave me a wonderful sister-in-law in Lucy and my nieces, Ava and Juliana, who make me the proudest aunt and fill my life up with endless joy.

And of course, my aunts, uncles, cousins, second cousins, third cousins, first cousins once removed, and everyone who shares a small amount of blood with me. A big thank-you as well to my in-laws, who I am not related to by blood (that would be awkward). I'm lucky my husband comes from such great stock.

Every child in school needs to feel like they matter, and I had so many teachers who gave me that security throughout my schooling. From Mrs. Edwards and Mrs. Hackett at Grazide Elementary, who nurtured my curiosity, to Mariam Samoniantz and Mrs. Malki at Mesrobian, who let me be myself, to Mr. Martin at Glen A. Wilson High in Hacienda Heights, who let me eat lunch in his room, and everyone in between.

Speaking of teachers, Liesel Reinhart, who I also mentioned in the book, not only gave me the courage to tackle public speaking but also gave me the idea to write this book. A big thank-you to Steve Seagle, who coached and co-wrote some of the best speeches I gave and helped me get over many of my fears.

Since working my first job at Burger King, I have been lucky enough to work with some incredible people who always looked out for me. Even my bosses at the Hollywood Bowl couldn't have been lovelier. Every gig I had taught me something important that I carried with me through every job I've had since. Along the way, I picked up lifelong friendships with many of my colleagues and managers. Work didn't feel like a chore as long as I was going into a workspace with these people.

I remember getting word from NBC's HR department that I would be working for Conan, and watched as Nate Kirtman, then a VP in the publicity department and one of my biggest cheerleaders, negotiated on my behalf for a bigger salary.

I remember Marc Liepis, who was a joy to work with before I ever got my job, telling me he texted Conan on my behalf right before my second interview.

I watched as some of my work peers went on to find their own partners in their personal lives—some got married, some had kids, some bought houses. We all became adults together and our friendship was always a constant.

A huge thanks to my Conan family—especially Jeff Ross (for his unending support), Mike Sweeney (for his genius behind the camera with the remotes I've been in as well as the Armenia episode), Matt O'Brien (for coming up with some of the best bits I've been involved in), Jason Chillemi (for always having my back), Adam Sachs (for trusting me to be a part of Conan's podcast), Matt Gourley (for being my ally and friend), Tracy King and Sarah Federowicz (for hiring me and much more).

I don't know where I'd be without my friends. From my best friends who I met in preschool and kindergarten to the new friends I picked up while filming at Largo during the

Covid pandemic, I've been so blessed with the greatest and most supportive people in the world. When I finished my shifts at Burger King, I'd drive to their houses to hang out. When I landed my internship at NBC, they celebrated with me at dinner. When I found out I would be working for Conan, they toasted along with me at a bar. When I signed my contract for this book, they bought me cupcakes and read my drafts. Special thank-yous to Christina Guerboian, Veronica Siranosian, Angineh Storino, Erin Levy, Meghan Sinclair, Erica Brown, Lindsay Sheehan, Meredith Fitzpatrick, April Lamb, and Brad Milison.

Thank you to Aaron Bleyaert, Ruthie Wyatt, Tiffany Roohani, Jessie Gaskell, and Gemma Paolo, and everyone at Team Coco for letting me use your photos for my insert. I'm terrible at capturing memories and without you I would have no way of remembering what I've been doing since 2009.

A big thank-you to the team at WME for all their help. Rick Rosen is too important and busy to help me but did anyway because he's a wonderful person. And a big thank-you to Suzanne Gluck and especially Andrea Blatt, who held my hand throughout this entire process. I would be an unmitigated disaster if it weren't for Andrea.

Thank you to Christopher Sabec and Jody Simon at Fox Rothschild LLP. Thanks for helping me through a process that would've otherwise frightened me.

To Cassidy Sachs and everyone at Plume—thank you for making my work coherent and being patient with me as I navigated writing a book while being a new mother. It was such a joy to work with all of you.

Having a brazen attitude to approach work like I do requires the knowledge that there will always be a safety net. I know there are so many people working now who don't have the freedom to act whatever way they'd like because they have no other choices. I personally know so many people who are in jobs that beat them down because they have mortgages and children and responsibilities that won't allow for them to act with a blatant disregard for authority. The courage I approached my career with was always rooted in the knowledge that I could always move back home, I could always ask the people I love for financial help, and I could always find a way to recover, because their support was always there if I ever needed it. There is legitimate power in knowing you're not alone and I will never forget how lucky I am.

With that said, I've told everyone I've ever had an informational with that we all deserve to feel like our voices are heard and that our opinions matter. I don't know where my career will lead me after Conan decides to retire, which I hope will be never, but I know I'll never settle for a job that'll have me dreading Mondays. I'll never be a *Cathy* cartoon.

Speaking of Conan, I am only including him in this acknowledgment because I feel like I have to, but this entire book is a big fat thank-you to him. From the moment he hired me, my life changed, and I'll spend the rest of it trying to find a way to pay him back for everything he's done for me.

And finally, I don't know how I lucked out to find the partner I did, but I could've never written this book without my husband's support and creativity. Tak, I love you so much and I'm so happy we made more humans together, and I know you hate public declarations of affection, but taking the late train home from Comic-Con in 2016 was the best decision I ever made. And Charlie and Mikey, you're both way too young to read this right now (or stand or walk), but I want you two to read this one day and know that I will always support any decision you make and will always be here as your safety net. I love you both, and being your mom has been the best gig I've ever had.

Whether you're working the drive-thru or assisting a legend (or being a legend yourself), I hope you find the satisfaction from working that I've been lucky to find. You deserve it. Everyone does. Even if we're the worst at what we do.